Hung Like a Seahorse

Seahorse

A Real-Life Transgender Adventure
of Tragedy, Comedy, and Recovery

D1516827

Hung Like a Seahorse

A Real-Life Transgender Adventure
of Tragedy, Comedy, and Recovery

By Quinn Alexander Fontaine

YouSpeakIt
PUBLISHING
The Easy Way
to Get Your Book
Done Right™

www.YouSpeakItPublishing.com

ISBN: 978-1-945446-10-8

Dedication

This book is lovingly dedicated to my teeny tiny family, Nancy Hewetson Cooke, Susan Cooke, and Raven Greene; to the best friends I could ever ask for, Sirena Irwin, Susan Mele; and to all my Tribesters, new and old. May we all continue to lead more authentic and fully embodied lives!

Acknowledgments

Along with my family of origin I must thank my family of choice: Michael Bernard Beckwith, Rickie Byars-Beckwith, and the entire Agape community; Debbie Fleischaker, Susan Mele, Sirena Irwin, Eliot Laurence, Shelley Pusich, Jan Boyer, Susan Marts, Lisa and Peter Munsat, Coco Mann, Julie Henderson Foran, Dr. Abby Braun, Daniela Fleischaker Suarez, Lara Suarez, David Goodman, DiaLuna Suarez Goodman, Cecile Lipworth, Liz Montoya, Jessica Montoya, Anastacio Trujillo, Carrie McCarthy, the Carney family, Marian Casey and family, Marion Tassin, Sarah Phipps, Taylor Massey, Jennifer Carr Munoz, Caroline Donnelly, Gaye Adegbalola, Leslie Ann Harty, Barbara Murphy, Abby Corbett, Laura Ferrazzano, Amber Alonso, Irenie Poitras, Anna Baker, Adrienne Freimuth, Aggie Damron, Alana Bader, Allan Swartzberg, Alicia Shelbourne, Allie Rivenbark, Drew Droege, Michael Coughlin, Mark and David Freeman, Amelia Edmondson, Amy Umberger, Andrea Maletta, Catherine Heymsfeld, Eileen Kerem, Annette Madrid, Anurati Kelly, Ashlee Preston, Matt Meadors, Ben Taxy, Stephanie Palmer Taxy, Beth and Joe Walkos, Betsy Burke, Kelly Murphy, Sunny Bak, Kassie Welch, Carrie Carlevaro, Mihaela Aurora, Carrie Neff, Kerry Cunningham, Stacey Eisner, Nathan Woodard, Stacy

Usie, Lisa Yedo, Cary Harrison, Chad Wold, Oona Bender, Chris Burke, Christina Yackery, Tara Duke, Emma Hill, Cindy Peters, Rebekah Wiggins, Cody Dove, Melissa Heiman, Danielle Romero, Daphne Brogdon, Deborah Sanford, Deirdre Salamone, Demian Baum, Diane Schneirer Perrin, Donna Harmon, Doug Montoya, Kristin Berg, Colleen Buchanan, Mara Malnekoff, Rebecca Babinski, Liz Mikola, Candace Kern, Jeff Luffey, Russ Canfield, Heidi Gall, Lucy Skully, Leon and Laurence Acord-Whiting, Jeannie Kahaney, Heidi Arnesen, Sandy Mooney, Ed Cheetham, Kate Hill, Eleanor Washington, Holly Chichester, Elise and Eric Gent, Ellen Borup, Kristen Klasky, Ester Brym, Kele and Fred McDaniel and family, Gaby Petrissans, Gail Daugherty, Geena Tommasi, Brian Mele, Hannah McPherson, Sasha Neulinger, Blyss Young, Heidi Ifft, Hilary Flower, Hudson McCall, Lynnannrose Miles, Lisa Rayner, Jerry Cheney, Sondra Sage, Roz, Atom Green, Polina Smutko, Jack and Nancy Arnold, Jacqui London, Monica Warden, Jade Shepard, Hazel Prejean, Jami Campbell, Tammy Hedge, Betty Richardson, Jane Biondi, Janice Evans, Jeff Friedman, Jen Steele, Lisa Muller-Jones, Jennifer and Vitorio Cristini, Jenoa Harlow, Jillian Brasch, Jody Booth, Julya Sembrat, John Angelos, John Meade, Azlan White, Teo Biele, Ana Gonzalez, Jonathan Lowe, Judea Eden, Carrie Baum, Julia Nutter, Juliet Brown, Juno Pitchford, Katie Crosman, Kenny Stanberry, Kimberly Miller, Laura

Loughry, Lauren Mora, Lianne Apointe, Rhea Maxwell, Lilly Marie, Linley Solari, Anika Solari, Brandon, Joaquin and Teya Rose, Lisa Russell, Lucy Brickey, Lyn Alicia Henderson, William "Mac" McCormack, Tracy Kelly, Malka Drucker, Maida Rogerson, Maria Rangel, Marianne Simpson, Mark Collin, Mary Alice Robinson, Mary Hoggard, Melissa Graskow, Mike Rose, Sarah Vato, Eric and Monica Oliver, Monte Monteleone, Morgana Rae, Nancie Lightner, Natalie Massenet, Neale and Gerry Smith, Noel Harvey, Pam and David Fleischaker, Joie Singer, Patty Brown, Pennel Bird, Kelly and Yas Molerio, Phoenix Simms, Shirley Klinghoffer, Rachel Reenstra, Randy Floyd, Renee Zisman, Roxy Andorfer, Ruthann Lentz, Brian Belefant, Sandi Stein, Sandra Pattison, Debra Doyle, Shar Jimenez, Shari Krauser, Simon Cain, Corey Smith, Sophia Kelly, Stephen and Josh Gill, Steve Silverman, Sue Russell, Suzanne Whang, Tanya Romero, Alice and Trevor Loy, Lee Cartwright, Vicky Virtuoso, Zane Stephens, Lara Jesser-Abell, Missy Ridge, Gaia Richards, Kieran McFarland, Kelly and Nana Owens, Sudarshan Ahben, Rachel Word, Janet Aerosmith, Roxy Buu, Jicari Hill, and Zelie Pollon.

Thanks to my agent, Tina Presley Borek.

And thanks to my team at YouSpeakIt Publishing: Maura Leon, Keith Leon, Nida Palpallatoc, Heather Taylor, and the editing team.

Contents

Introduction

Hi.

My name is Quinn.

I'm a recovering humanoid. I'm a recovering sex and love addict, alcoholic, and drug addict. I'm also a survivor of pre-verbal childhood sexual abuse at the hands of my father. I'm a trans guy who is almost two years into his transition. I'm a recovering humanoid.

"Hi, Quinn!"

Hi, guys. Thanks for picking up this book. I'm absolutely humbled that I get to speak directly to you right here, right now. Today, as I write, is actually March 30, 2016. I'm forty-eight years old. It has taken me this long, which is the perfect timing, to decide to get fully embodied and BE on this planet.

Yes, I still have a lot more work to do, but don't we all?

The issue is whether we are doing our work or not. I have met a lot of people who are sleepwalking, who aren't super-conscious, or aren't conscious at all, and are simply going through the motions in their lives. They are not investigating or questioning their purpose.

This is a book about doing the work. This is a book about the nitty-gritty of my life, about why it took me so long to come into my body temple, how hard it's been, and how joyous it's been to surrender and do all my healing work to recover from childhood trauma and multiple addictions and fully accept being transgender. The healing work is ongoing. Getting back to my essence has been the stinkiest and most beautiful gift I've ever given myself.

I found comedy and humor early on. Thank God I did because otherwise I'd be in jail because of the rage that accompanies the feelings of being lost and confused and not wanted, not seen, and not identifiable.

Ultimately, what I'm trying to share is that we each have a story, and we are *not* our story. So many of us get trapped by thinking we are less than others or unlovable or that we should not be taking up space altogether.

I'm here to remind you that you are here for a reason. There's only one of you in the entire cosmos. All you have to do is be true to your essence and your calling and your gifts and talents.

To be 100 percent transparent, I wrote this book because of the help available to get it done. I met Keith Leon and his wife Maura twenty years ago at the Agape International Spiritual Center in Los Angeles,

California. I decided then and there that I'd work with them someday. The right time came about when I was struggling to put pen to paper or fingers to keyboard while writing my next one-person show. Because I was feeling stuck creatively, I thought I should go down this path, with all the support offered by YouSpeakIt Publishing.

I've learned that when I'm blocked in one direction, it's possible to find another way to communicate my energy, to be creative, and to be expressive.

I've needed to write this book. It has led me to deeper healing, and it has reminded me that I'm an artist. Art can flow in all kinds of ways. I hope that rings true for you, as well, and you might even put the book down right now and start finger painting or dancing.

There are lots of ways to read this book for the best results. Whether you're a chef or you only cook for yourself at home, you're going to want to gently cover this book in flour and then melt down two tablespoons of butter, unsalted, pour it over the book, and put it in the oven 350 degrees for ten minutes. Just kidding.

Are you sleepwalking, or did you get that?

You got that. I know you did.

The only direction I have for you is to read this only if you want to. If my words don't resonate with you, or if you don't want to read, then give it (or regift it) to someone else. Someone, somewhere may need to read this. I'm really writing from my heart. We are all heart-based, spiritual beings having a human experience.

I picked up Eckhart Tolle's bestseller, *A New Earth: Awakening to Your Life's Purpose*, on several occasions, and none of his writing made sense. I'm not comparing myself to him; I'm simply saying that in different times of our lives, different writings and teachings will resonate. Whether you stay with me throughout this book or not, it's not very long, so keep it on the bookshelf for later. I guarantee you that at some point in your life it will speak to you.

Read it at your own pace. Reread it if you need to. If you need to put this book down right now and sign up for a marathon, do so. That is a form of art. And my message to you is that your body is your vehicle and conduit.

I hope you gain ten pounds from this book. Just kidding! I hope you gain a sense of freedom by reading this book. I hope that you gain a sense of truth-telling because then you can set yourself free, and in doing so, you give others permission to do the same. I hope you laugh a few times. I hope that if you have any healing to do for yourself, you find a supportive way to do that. The more we heal ourselves, the more we heal the planet. I know this to be true.

If at any point you get scared or overwhelmed, put the book down. Pick up the phone, call a friend, and tell them what is coming up for you. So many of us tend to isolate ourselves. It's not just addicts who do this — most of us prefer hiding to reaching out.

How many of us know our neighbors?

If you don't know your neighbors, go meet them. After this writing session, I'll go out and meet a spiritual being having a human experience in my neighborhood whom I haven't met before.

Deal? Deal.

Welcome, and I hope you enjoy this book!

CHAPTER ONE

Transgender
Reality While Growing Up

LONELINESS AND CONFUSION

The loneliness and confusion that I experienced is not something I have experienced alone. Most transgender people have felt this throughout the ages, even now that *transgender* is a word. The suicide rate among trans people is the highest among all demographics—including combat veterans—and that speaks volumes. That screams loudly that this population is still hurting. I'm speaking directly to this so that someone out there can know that they are not alone.

The Word *Transgender* Did Not Exist

While I was growing up in the late 1970s in rural Virginia, there were no images or articles about trans people—the word *transgender* didn't even exist. I was starved to see someone like me. Of course, I saw people, like a gay couple in town or someone who was a lesbian, or at least I imagined that they were gay. But nobody was speaking up openly about being gay, bisexual, or anything other than straight in those days.

About once a year there would be news coverage of the gay and lesbian March on Washington, but I'd look at the people in the crowd and know intuitively that they were not *my* people. They are close to being a tribe I could join, but not really. I was a straight boy in a girl's body.

I went to school from kindergarten through twelfth grade in Fredericksburg, Virginia. When I graduated, I knew I had to leave town to go to college. It wasn't about getting a great education. I needed to find a safe city where I could find my people. I chose Boston. That was in the late 1980s. And even at that time, the word *transgender* still didn't exist in mainstream culture.

"You'd Be So Cute If Only You Were a Boy"

I felt an exquisite pain when a girl that I had a crush on would say, "God, you'd be so cute if only you were a boy."

Of course, I couldn't respond honestly. I didn't have the courage or the language, but I used to fantasize about saying, "Close your eyes and let's fucking pretend."

I had crushes on girls from as early as I can remember. In third grade, I fell in love with a first-grader, and all through school I had the same feelings toward her. She was always sweet to me. She could tell I adored her because I turned twenty shades of red every time I saw her. She knew what was going on. She was never mean. I called her before I left for college, confessing my love big time.

I said, "If we never see each other again, you have to know I love you."

But I remember in particular what occurred at a roller-skating rink called Skateland. I was there with my younger sister. I was probably in fourth grade, and she was in second grade.

A little girl waiting in line at the crappy snack center asked my sister, "Is that your brother? He is so cute."

I stood up straight in the best posture I had ever had in my life. I felt *seen*.

My sister quickly said, "No, that is my sister." My posture went from ten to one. But I'll never forget that moment because I lived for little moments like that.

It was at about that age, fourth grade, when they began to separate the boys and girls in gym class. I didn't know where to go.

What side of the gym did I belong on?

This was an internal feeling. I never voiced it. None of my feelings could be voiced at home or at school because there was no container for my questions. There was no safety net. The gay kids didn't have a safe place, either. But I was trans. No one knew what to do with that.

If I went to the grocery store by myself, the grocery clerk would say, "Here you are, son," and it would be one of those moments when someone recognized me and I felt that I was not crazy and other people could see who I was and feel my male energy.

Even my cousin, who is ten years younger than me, would say, using my birth name, "When Kathleen comes back over, can he help me build a tree house?"

My aunt and uncle would have to gently guide her to use the *proper* pronoun. I was never embarrassed by those moments because it told me that people were reading my energy. Little kids especially always thought that I was a boy. They aren't yet indoctrinated with the cultural rules about how boys are supposed to do this and girls are supposed to do that.

Puberty

Puberty was absolute hell. I was a year-round swimmer. The girls' swimming uniform was made of a Lycra that grabbed every curve and nuance of my budding female form. It was fucking ridiculous. I continued to swim because I loved the sport. When I started developing breasts, my posture became a nightmare. I began hunching over, trying to hide the fact that my body was deceiving my male brain.

Getting my period at age eleven was the most intense and scary thing that I could remember happening to me up until that time. I don't remember my childhood before age eleven, and my childhood trauma didn't rear its ugly head until my late thirties. Never mind the fact that I had never really been told about it. When they showed us a film in school with a little bit of information about going through puberty, I was dissociated. I didn't want to watch the film while sitting with a group of girls. It was so embarrassing. I couldn't relate. I couldn't believe that my body was going to behave like that, so there was a disconnect between my reality and what I was being taught.

Because I grew up with no images that looked like me, there were no role models. I wondered if I were the only one on the planet. Many trans kids wonder this even today, especially kids in isolated rural areas.

I went on a high school senior trip with my class to New York City. I was walking past a shopping mall near the piers and saw a man and a woman in a store. They both looked like they might be gay.

I wrote a note, walked by the store, and dropped the note. It was a cry for help.

It said:

You guys seem cool.

I'm a gay kid. (I didn't know the correct words yet, so I used *gay* instead of *trans.*)

There are no other people in my hometown like this. Will you please call me?

I left my phone number for two random people in New York City. They never found the note. They never called me. Maybe they did find the note. Maybe they ate it thinking it was a protein snack.

Who knows?

I was always looking for my tribe and trying to connect in random ways. I even wrote a letter to the music group Berlin. I wrote them a letter about my pain and sadness. I didn't hear back, but that's okay. Maybe Berlin made a group protein snack out of my letter, too. We need to honor that everybody has different dietary requirements.

BEING IN THIS BODY

I fully believe that we are all spiritual beings having a human experience. I also believe that we choose our experiences based on the lessons we need to learn and the things that will help our soul unfold. Having said that, I also believe that we often choose harder paths than we seemingly can manage.

I definitely chose some hard stuff. I chose to have a soul contract with my father in which sexual abuse would be an issue in childhood. I also chose to be transgender. I was unable to be naturally at ease in my body, and my body was shut down from trauma. There was a disconnect from my brain, and that was extra challenging.

I share these memories because there is hope. Feeling natural and at ease is possible. Full integration of mind, body, and spirit is a reality.

I Was a Cute, Vivacious, and Free Little Guy

I don't remember my childhood before age eleven because of childhood trauma. I have pieced it together through photographs.

My sister often says, "Remember when...?"

I respond, "No, I wasn't there."

She pulls out a photograph, and there I am. I don't remember the day. I don't remember the place. I don't remember the activities. I don't remember the clothes I'm wearing.

In doing so, I have looked at hundreds of photographs. Thank goodness my mom was a photographer and took lots of photographs. In the photos, I'm the cutest little guy on the planet.

There's one photo in particular, taken when I was four years old. I'm rockin' some serious sideburns.

I've asked my mom, "What's up with the photo of me with the sideburns?" She doesn't really have an answer.

She says, "I don't know. I guess the neighbor cut your hair."

I ask, "Mom, who told the neighbor I wanted sideburns cut into my hair?"

Me as a four-year-old with sideburns. The crazy thing about this photo is that nobody knows who gave me the haircut or who requested the sideburns. This is yet another mystery moment from my childhood captured on film.

What happened?

Did I randomly show up at a neighbor's house and say, "Hi, I'm four years old, and I'm trapped in the wrong body. Please help me look more like the boy I am."? Or did I say something like, "Hi, you don't know me but I need your help. I've got some kickass cheekbones, and I think sideburns will really help the little ladies in preschool notice me more."?

I was a vivacious, energetic little guy. There is no doubt that my energy was full-on boy. Part of me was choosing to be my true self all along. To this day, I'm an optimist, and I still choose life. That, in itself, is a miracle.

When It Became Crystal Clear That My Penis Didn't Get Lost in the Mail

In fifth grade, when all the kids started pseudo-dating, there were after-school dances, which were awkward as hell. I was pubescent and uncomfortable in my body, and all I wanted to do was ask a cute girl to dance.

When I wasn't at school, I was being a producer at home and in the neighborhood. Friends would want to play, and I'd insist we play Boyfriend and Girlfriend, so I could be a boy and act out my fantasies.

Or we would play *Happy Days*, and I'd be the Fonz.

Need I say more?

At a certain age, other girls would only allow me to act out being a girl. They didn't understand why we would be playing boyfriend and girlfriend when there were no boys there. I was crushed. This new rule took away my only honest, gender-based expression.

It didn't stop me from having crushes on girls. I remember one girl in particular that I had a crush on—who will remain nameless—and the exact moment that she told me about her first boyfriend. I was devastated.

He may have been cute, but he wasn't funny or sweet, like me.

I had to bear all this heartbreak with no one and nowhere to talk about it. I didn't write normal, angst-ridden teenage poems. I didn't have that outlet.

Besides, what if I had condensed everything into early, anguished, transgender haikus?

There was the absolute horror of someone potentially finding them.

I got my period when I was eleven years old. That was absolutely horrific to me, and it was all happening way too fast. Before that, I could stay in denial about being a girl, even though I was growing small breasts. When I got my period, it felt as though I could no longer dream and pretend that I was a boy. I'd go to sleep most nights praying that I'd wake up male.

Obviously, I didn't know how boys' and girls' bodies worked if I was imagining that I could magically have a penis. This is a pretty common experience that I hear about from my trans brothers and sisters. We were all in that much pain, and we all imagined that our bodies could and would eventually change to match our brains.

Moving From Self-Hatred to Self-Love

I remember very clearly being in the shower in Los Angeles in 1997, after having just moved there. I was thirty years old, shaving my legs, doing the *normal* female thing. I caught myself sending all kinds of negative energy to my vagina. I was cursing it in my head, and even a few words came out loud. I had the wherewithal at that time to stop.

Even if I feel that way, it's not healthy, I thought. I'm going to manifest some kind of funky cancer or something because I'm throwing so much hate in that direction. I should change that up, even if I don't fully believe it. I need to balance that energy and go toward the positive.

I started saying out loud:

- *I love you.*
- *I accept you.*
- *I forgive you.*
- *I'm sorry.*

I was apologizing to my genitals. It felt both weird and completely necessary.

At that time, I didn't know I had preverbal childhood sexual trauma. I had no idea why I hated my genitals so much. Granted, the transgender piece brings that up for a lot of us. I've hated my body because of being trans. I've denied and been embarrassed about it, but the disgust, hate, and venomous energy that I was spewing at my vagina was originally caused by childhood sexual abuse. Growing up transgender, though, at the time I did, was another form of body-based trauma. For me, they are both enmeshed, like a locked fist. I didn't know what came first, the trauma or transgender, because the intersectionality of them is so complex.

I had the wherewithal to observe my attitude and change it. Some part of me knew to soften up, even if I didn't fully believe what I was saying. I could move from self-hate to self-love.

Childhood sexual trauma also carried over into my romantic life and my sex life. I've slept with approximately 107.5 women. To my mind, that is a lot of sexual encounters. But I could do it only with drugs and alcohol. Sober sex is a whole different gig.

At this moment, I'm almost two-and-a-half years into testosterone hormone treatment. I've been landing slowly the whole time, mind and body coming into alignment. I'd say that in the last six months, I have finally come home to myself. I'm finally in my body temple. From this place, all things are possible.

A friend saw me walking down the street the other day in Santa Fe and texted me right away:

I just saw you walking to your truck. You're fully embodied. I have never seen you or experienced you like that.

It felt great to have someone mirror that back to me. I actually feel different in my body and the way I occupy space. From this place, there's a calm and a peace that I've never experienced before in my life. So much can happen from this place of embodiment and self-empowerment.

FROM PAIN TO POWER

I'm writing about this specifically because I have learned as an Underdog — by the way, I love that cartoon — that there is power in pain. We can transform pain into power. We can transform hiding into being seen and taking up space on the planet without apology. I've done that, and I know other people can do it, too. The only catch is that there is work involved.

I want to speak to anyone out there who is hurting or thinks they are alone or thinks it's not safe to be in this world in the body that they are in. It's safe, but it takes work to claim that safety and to give ourselves the gift of knowing we belong here.

As Michael Bernard Beckwith says, "We are an on-purpose with purpose."

Today, I know that to be more true than ever before.

Michael is one of my spiritual mentors and the founder of the Agape International Spiritual Center. I credit Agape, my humor, and my friends and family with helping me learn to stay on the planet.

Finding My Sense of Humor

Transgender didn't exist as a word when I was growing up so I didn't know what to call myself. In hindsight, I'll say that as a trans kid, I knew I was different. I also knew I was different because I grew up super-lower-middle-class. I knew that was a factor as well. Because I felt so different, on some level I felt unlovable. I know now that the *unlovability* that I've held as a core belief was mainly due to the trauma and abuse I suffered at the hands of my father.

I'll never forget my first joke. It was the first time I felt powerful. It was in third grade. The teacher had us all sitting on the floor, and she was sitting in a chair reading to us. The subject of the Statue of Liberty came up.

She asked, "Boys and girls, who knows what it says on the tablet that she's holding?"

I quickly raised my hand.

The teacher called on me: "Kathleen?"

"It says, *Made in France!*"

The smart kids laughed. She looked at me, and I could tell she felt that I stole her thunder. She didn't like it. I was told to go stand in the small trashcan for a little while because I was disruptive and being a smart aleck. I didn't care that I was in trouble because I knew it was a great joke. I knew it was smart and clever and different. It took everybody out of the moment and made them laugh. I'll never forget that.

It was the first time I felt the power of what humor can do. Humor is a unifier. I use it as a unifier. I don't use humor and comedy as a way to separate and make fun of others. I make fun of the human condition so we can all laugh together. After all, we're way more alike than we are different.

I Had a Better Understanding of Both Genders Than Most People

Growing up knowing I was a boy in the wrong body, I closely studied both genders. I started studying even more when the division of genders happened in the gym.

I think I really started studying them because I felt loneliness and rejection. It wasn't even outright rejection by other people; I was loved. I got that. But if I were loved by a girl, why wouldn't she date me?

School and society were heterosexual. Life was heterosexual. I knew I didn't fall into that schematic because of the body I was in. I always knew that I was a straight guy. That was more of the confusion piece, and it caused a deep sadness.

There were a few women I dated casually over the years who told me it was brave for me to follow my heart.

In essence, they were telling me that they weren't brave enough to follow their hearts. If they were more courageous, we could be together. That speaks to society and the power that fear has over a lot of people.

I entered treatment at the Life Healing Center in Santa Fe, New Mexico, on April 12, 2006.

During the core process group one morning, a man said, "Women have it easier."

I responded, "Wait, time out. Can we talk about this?"

I turned to the women in the group and said, "What do you think? Do men or women have it easier?"

All the women said, "Men have it easier."

Women believe men have it easier, and men believe women have it easier. This is a huge conversation that needs to happen on our planet and in our culture specifically. If that is happening, and even if people aren't speaking about it but still are acting based on that belief system, then that is a factor of separation.

I was the only person in the room who spoke up about it, saying I could see both sides. I got why both sides think this way.

The men couldn't understand what the women thought, and the women couldn't understand what the men thought. It was a clear moment that taught me that I'm in the middle. I *do* understand both genders.

At this point of my transition, I feel more like a man. I still do not feel comfortable owning the word *man* for myself. I feel comfortable saying I'm a trans guy. At some point, I'll be comfortable saying I'm a man. But at this time, it does not feel 100 percent right.

In my transition, I've been embraced by both men and women. I've been most surprised by how men have been loving and accepting and nurturing with me. It's blowing my mind, actually.

There's an exchange that happens between men, and sometimes it's spoken, in which they check in with each other.

I have heard so many guys in the world, sometimes strangers, ask, "What's up, bro? You good?"

Yeah, I'm good. It's been a really healing transition.

Moving In and Out of All Circles

It's time for a disclaimer: The one group I have never felt comfortable with is big groups of jocks. When all the athletes hang out together, I do not feel comfortable or safe, but when I meet a jock one-on-one, I can get him laughing and having a good time. This says something about men, or boys, in groups.

By making jokes and doing characters, I can make people laugh, which is a great way to disarm them, or to get them to be more open. That is the gift of humor.

Being trans and different led me to use humor as a safety device. I definitely knew it was a safety mechanism on some level, and it was also a defense mechanism when needed. Humor alone can bridge so many gaps. I love that. Even though I was kind of a loner in a lot of ways, I was also very popular. It was a weird mix.

I think I've been more highly sexual than a lot of people. This doesn't mean I actually had sex, but rather that I engaged people with my sexual energy, and that energy was also my creative energy, from the same chakra area. I think I was seeking out positions of power, even if not in outright ways.

CHAPTER TWO

Addiction, Trauma, and Mental Lack of Wellness

LIVING AN ALL-OR-NOTHING LIFE

Astrologers have told me that I have three strong aspects in Scorpio. I know my birth sign is Scorpio. That is one reason I live with an all-or-nothing attitude. But I'm an addict through and through with addictive behaviors that showed up as early as I can remember. That is another reason I have lived all-or-nothing, black or white. I never knew the grey until much later in life.

We hear about little inner-city kids who think their only way out of the ghetto is to make it into the NFL. They are dreaming of being professional ball players not because it's their passion, but because they think it's their ticket out. Their families are telling them that this is the case. That is one little example of all-or-nothing thinking.

This kind of attitude permeates society and keeps people from following their true passions because they are not even encouraged to explore what their passions are. Everybody is looking for a quick fix. I know for myself that this has been true for most of my life. I'm still working on these issues of extremism.

Perfectionism

I remember perfectionism showing up in my life fairly early on. One of the clearest memories I have is acting in one of my school's plays and rehearsing at home alone. I tried to get my lines perfect before the first rehearsal, and I did the best I possibly could so that no one would see me fall on my face, so to speak, or struggle with the process.

I carried that mindset over into a lot of things. I remember a time when I hadn't studied for a test. I was a senior, but I was taking an eighth-grade science class because it had become available and counted as a credit.

I thought: *Well, let's take Easy Street.*

I hadn't studied for the test, and I didn't know a single answer. Instead of turning in an empty paper, I put down random answers that had nothing to do with Earth Science. The teacher turned my paper over to the guidance counselor, and I was called in for a psychiatric evaluation.

This was an example of all-or-nothing perfectionism. I couldn't earn a score of one hundred on this paper, and I was not going to accept an F, so I chose to fuck around with society and everything else. I didn't realize I was going to scare people, but apparently I did with my bizarre answers.

I'm still working with my tendency for all-or-nothing because it shows up all the time in my thinking. It doesn't help that the energetic mantra of *bigger, faster, famous, yesterday* is what's selling or pushing everything.

If you missed it, then fuck you.

Everyone is trying to win the game, but the game is not winnable, because the game we are playing is wrong. Let's bring it back to living our lives and realizing that ultimately we are perfect, whole, and complete.

To relax into this truth is liberating. However, very few of us know how to relax, and I'm at the top of that list.

Going-Away Party

I'm infamous for not showing up at a going-away party that was thrown in my honor.

This happened right before I moved from San Francisco to Los Angeles. Being the country mouse that I am, San Francisco seemed to be a city of the right size. The thought of Hollywood and Los Angeles scared me. I had starred in *Some Prefer Cake*, an independent gay-girl feature film, and it felt as though if I didn't go to Hollywood at that time, I'd never go. Everything was in alignment. The move was happening.

My boss at the catering company was planning a going-away party for me. I also had a stand-up comedy show that night at a local club. Too much was happening at once. I was overwhelmed, and I did what I always did. I shut down.

Instead of figuring out a way to navigate the party and give everyone my best without being depleted, I did nothing. I went to bed. I didn't call to cancel the stand-up gig. I didn't call to say I was sick or overwhelmed and that I didn't know how to show up to the party. I didn't know how to tell the truth, nor ask for help. I just went to sleep. That was all I was able to do in that moment.

There have been many moments in my life when I have opted to lie down and do nothing. I just can't deal with everything, so I go to sleep. A friend in college joked about how I slept through a whole semester. The crazy thing was, she was right. I *did* sleep through the whole semester. Talk about anxiety and being overwhelmed — that much sleep with no drugs, just depression. If sleep were a bank, I'd be able to give everybody millions of minutes. That's one thing I'm trying to do differently now: get up and face my life daily. I'm learning to live life on life's terms.

It's an interesting story, but I do feel some shame for the fact that I didn't show up to a going-away party. I did make amends and acknowledge what was going on with me. Confessing clears up the situation a bit. Making amends is a powerful gift I give myself.

At the same time, I was left thinking: *Why is this my skillset? Why is that the best I could do in that situation?*

I made peace with it. I'm trying to do everything better than that now, and I'm doing a pretty good job.

It has been a long and winding road back to being my true self on many fronts.

Geographic Stress

My dad was in the military and put in for reassignment every six months to a year. Before I was six years old, we had moved eight times. I was born in the Philippines, and then we moved all over the world, finally landing in Fredericksburg, Virginia. That is where I spent my formative years, from kindergarten through twelfth grade.

It's no surprise after my childhood that, as an adult, it has taken me a long time to feel settled. For example, I lived in Los Angeles for ten years and stayed in thirteen different places. One apartment, so to speak, was a sailboat, and I never learned to sail.

There is a part of me that thinks: *I'm now just learning that it's okay to be me in the fullest sense and to express myself in my fullness in all areas, whatever they may be — my happiness, my sadness, my rage — as long as it's truthful and not hurting anyone.*

Early in life I believed what a lot of people were telling me, that I was too much to handle.

Maybe you've heard the same things:

- You're too much.
- You're too intense.
- You're too dramatic
- You're too sensitive.

Some part of me is still healing from that. What I now know to be true is that if someone is telling me I'm too much of anything, it's simply that — I'm too much of that thing for *them*. Not for me. Not for my Tribesters. This has been a great lesson.

There is still a part of me that thinks: *If I'm going to be big and have big feelings, then I need to leave and move.*

That's not really a solution. It's time to trust that right where I am is right where I need to be. I am a work in progress.

RECOVERING FROM CHILDHOOD TRAUMA

I'm a childhood sexual abuse survivor, and thirty-seven years passed before I knew this.

I'm sharing this because we meet so many people who look as though they are sleepwalking, and often there is a reason for this. I don't know the exact statistics worldwide, but I think the numbers in the United States are that one of every four girls and one of every six boys is sexually abused before they turn eighteen (National Sexual Violence Resource Center, *www.nsvrc.org*). The numbers are staggering.

That sexual assault can happen to this number of children speaks to the power of dissociation.

It speaks to the power of the organism, the body itself, trying to protect:

- Itself
- The soul
- The mind
- The emotional system

The neurological system of a trauma survivor suffers. More and more is being done to map the connections between trauma and addiction and the cycle of abuse. Most trauma survivors are not able to stop the cycle. I'm very happy and proud to say that in my family, it stops with my sister and me. We were both abused by my dad. It stops with us.

I knew something was weird for me. If I was touched in certain ways, I'd shut down. I ended up bawling and crying if I had sex in certain ways. I was trying to rationalize all along that I was just really sensitive, or I felt extra close to the person I was with.

At one point, I even asked my therapist, "Don't most men cry after sex?"

She replied, "Not in my understanding of it, and not based on what I've heard over the years."

I was always trying to make it okay. I was trying to find a reason why it was happening to me.

I didn't learn the truth until I went on a trip with my dad when I was thirty-seven years old. Cellular memory kicked in, and everything started to make sense.

Two therapists later told me that I don't remember my childhood before eleven. I have these weird incidents when I'm touched in certain ways, and this happened with my dad. They said it sounded like possible childhood trauma.

The minute they said that, I arrived back in my body. I had been dissociated after that vacation. Just being in my father's presence on a daily basis, never mind that we were on a trip, was enough to stir up cellular memory.

A Trip With My Dad

I hadn't been on a trip with my dad in eons. He called me out of the blue and invited me to go on a trip to the Bermuda Triangle with his girlfriend and another friend. I said yes because nothing was happening in my life. I was living on a sailboat. Stand-up comedy was not happening. The catering season was slow. A girlfriend had just broken up with me.

There was also a hopeful feeling that I could heal something with my dad. I didn't know what needed to heal, but I knew that we had a weird relationship, and he had not been able to be in my life for years. That longing part of me still wished I had a dad.

So, the trip was fine. But I started drinking more than usual. Some part of me was really disturbed. I drank nightly on the cruise ship. I befriended the gay cruise director, and we had a blast every night.

It wasn't until I was flying back home to Los Angeles that I felt a pit of overwhelming sadness. Where was home? Why was I going to LA? Nothing was happening there. I always thought home is where the heart is. I didn't have a girlfriend at the time, although I usually was in a relationship, which was part of my sex and love addiction.

When I got home, it all escalated. I had a dissociative experience. I acted out with my ex-girlfriend. I called her and scared her to the point where she went to court and was awarded a three-year restraining order against me. It wasn't until I contacted a friend and talked with a therapist that I got back into my body. I knew all along this had nothing to do with my ex-girlfriend. In that moment, it was very clear. This was rage and discomfort from having just spent time with my dad.

All my triggers finally made sense.

I finally understood why I didn't remember my childhood. I blocked it. I was most likely in a mild to moderate dissociative state for most of my childhood. I remember sucking my thumb and twirling my hair with my other hand. I watched TV at my grandparents' house and started zoning out to the point that when my mom came to pick my sister and me up, she would have to cut my hair to get my fingers free. No one ever questioned this.

Nobody ever asked why I was sucking my thumb, tranced out, and twirling my fingers in my hair until the circulation cut off.

My mom just dutifully cut off the knot and freed my fingers.

Nobody seemed to know why or when I started sucking my thumb. To this day, I'll suck my thumb guilt-free. It's the only thing that soothes me or helps ground me after a huge post-traumatic stress disorder (PTSD) flare up.

The way I'd act out sexually combined with the way I'd respond to any rape scene in a film screamed that something must have happened to me.

I didn't make that connection. I just thought I was super sensitive. I'm a humanitarian. I care about people. I don't want anyone to be raped. Men or women. I never thought that sexual assault had happened to me.

So many things started to make sense.

Therapy

I had been to therapy on and off for a few years. This was not super intense therapy, but rather I was trying to learn behavior modifications, trying to figure out how to be in the world consistently, trying to not go to sleep for weeks on end, and so on. After the trip with my dad, I met a new therapist right away. I was seeing her three times a week. It was intense. I'd be in deep despair every session, but a lot of stuff came to light. In that time frame, we did EMDR, which is Eye Movement Desensitization and Reprocessing. It's an incredibly powerful form of therapy. I began to recall and reframe multiple abuse experiences with my dad. So much started to make sense.

About three months into therapy three times a week, in a hypnosis session, an image of me as a baby in diapers came up. I didn't even want to know what the next scene was going to be, so my higher self stepped in and stopped the process, shut it down.

Shelley, my therapist told me, "I just witnessed you shut down completely."

I told her I was glad I did. I couldn't handle those images.

That night, I got online looking for sex. This was how I was going to handle my emotions. I was going to fuck them out and away. I found a woman's ad, asking to act out a consensual rape scene, something I'd never even thought of doing before.

I'll never forget driving north on the 405 with my huge strap-on jutting down my pant leg. I felt completely alive, on edge, and full of terror. I couldn't believe I was actually going to do this. I was driving to a total stranger's home. I was going to act out a consensual rape scene. What the actual fuck?

As planned, she left the front door unlocked. I found her sleeping on the floor by the fireplace. I just stood there, staring at her for a bit. She must have felt me, and she startled awake. In that moment, I knelt down as she sat up. I gave her the sweetest kiss I could. I wanted her to know that I was safe. We were about to do some crazy-assed shit, and I was safe.

We did the dirty deed, and then she asked, "Do you want to do some coke?

I said, "I hate that drippy thing in the back of the throat."

She said, "Do you want to smoke it?"

I said, "Yeah, okay."

Not one part of me was thinking: *WARNING – You're supposed to say no to crack and to heroin.* Not one part of me gave a fuck.

If I was thinking anything, it was: *Fuck life!*

When you smoke crack, you lose track of time like nobody's business. We were just smoking, fucking, and talking. But suddenly I remembered that I had to get ready for a therapy appointment in two hours. I was able to drive there on time. But it was obvious that I was high, and that I was not trying to hide anything.

I said, "Shelley, I can't do this intense trauma therapy and smoke crack cocaine at the same time. I'm gonna go smoke crack. I'll call you when I'm done."

She replied, "Kathleen, do you have any idea what you're saying? Do you even get how dangerous that drug is?"

I said, "Yeah, I do, and I don't fuckin' care. I really don't care. I don't want to come in here and deal with images of me as a baby in fucking diapers. I can't go there. I can't even comprehend that reality. I'll call you when I'm done."

I moved in with my consensual-rape-scene partner, trust-fund baby, instant girlfriend. We proceeded to smoke crack for a year and three months straight. After six months of smoking crack, I was trying to die. I'd take a huge puff and hold it in and watch my skinny body respond, the veins pulsing very slowly. To the best of my knowledge, no one has committed suicide by holding their breath. I thought I was going to be the first.

At the end of that run, I knew I needed help. It had been a year and three months of nonstop drinking, fucking, and crack-smoking.

I called Shelley just like I said I would, and said, "I can't seem to die. I don't know how to live. What's next?"

"Rehab's next," she said.

Naked and high as hell, I got online and typed: *multiple addictions preverbal childhood sexual abuse HELP* into the Google search bar.

The answer: *The Life Healing Center: Intensive Trauma Resolution.*

My whole body responded with a YES.

I knew instantly that's where I needed to go to begin my healing journey.

The Life Healing Center (LHC) is in Santa Fe, New Mexico. I'd been to Santa Fe once before and really liked it. After missing two rescheduled flights, I was finally able to put the crack pipe down and make it onto the plane. I spent three months in intensive therapy there. I'd never even heard of sex and love addiction until I got to LHC.

They told me I was off the charts for sex and love addiction.

So not only would I be in recovery from addiction to alcohol, pills, pot, shopping, dangerous behaviors, and food: I had to add sex and love to the seemingly ever-growing list.

LHC is a major treatment center for trauma and multiple addictions. I checked myself in on April 12, 2006.

I tell people if they come to Santa Fe to heal and don't heal, then they really don't want to.

Every modality of healing exists in Santa Fe. There is a high level of consciousness here, too, among a lot of people. It's a wonderful town. There are also a lot of great meetings, leading to a lot of great recovery.

I succeeded in getting one year clean and sober. Then I started chronically relapsing with pills, pot, and alcohol. Shortly thereafter, I began stealing my partner's pain pills and abusing my prescription sleep medication.

All the while, the addict inside my head kept justifying my use by telling me: *Hey, it's not crack cocaine; you're good!*

One day, after being sick and tired of being sick and tired, I responded: *No, I'm not good. I'm not good at all. It's time to get real about all of this. If millions of other people can get 100 percent clean and sober, why can't I?*

April 12, 2006, is my original clean date. I never went back to smoking crack. I've also worked a strong program in my sex and love addiction. With only one small exception —she shall remain nameless—I've only experienced healthy intimacy. That in itself is a huge win.

It took me years to finally clean up everything else. With my doctor's help, I weaned myself off the copious amounts of Xanax I had been abusing. My last drunken night was the Wednesday before Thanksgiving, 2015. I put myself under my version of house arrest on Thanksgiving and through the following day.

I knew if I left my loft, I'd go buy alcohol. I stayed home. I stayed safe. I got sober. On that Saturday and Sunday, I went to three recovery meetings a day. Slowly but surely, I started putting clean and sober days together, one day at a time.

Most days have been really easy, but the hard days have been incredibly challenging. I continue to be in therapy, doing trauma healing. I've been in therapy almost consistently for almost twelve years.

I really wish, as a lot of people do, that there was a point in healing and recovery at which I could say:

- I'm done.
- I'm healed.
- I'm fully recovered.

There is no finish line with a crowd cheering for our triumph and winning time. Instead there is the daily victory of choosing life on life's terms, moment by moment. We have to heal and recover for ourselves first and foremost.

A lot of people describe the healing and recovery process as peeling the layers of the proverbial onion.

I much prefer likening it to peeling the layers of an artichoke.

Why?

Because there is a heart in the middle of an artichoke. I don't know where I first heard that saying, but it stayed with me. That's what I'm working on: moment by moment and day by day, doing my best, being in the world, and being as much of a beneficial presence as I can be. My work every day is to be authentic, stay clean and sober, and play it forward.

Once I made the decision to begin my transition from female to male, my entire nervous system began to calm down. Now there's an alignment of my mind and body that I never knew was possible. So much more life energy can flow through me now that I'm feeling more at home in my body temple. I can also be more heart-based than ever before. It's finally safe to be myself — my *full* self.

I attribute my decision to transition with being able to finally get and stay clean and sober.

I've heard stories about people not getting in touch with their trauma, and some are even older than I am. I believe that memories and traumas don't present themselves until we're able and willing to work with them. For some people, that may mean they're in their seventies and eighties. I've heard stories about people who live their whole lives and have no clue why they react certain ways to certain things. But later on they get real and find out, or a relative on his or her deathbed tells them the truth about their family or their childhood.

My point is that it's never too late. As your path opens up, trust it. You will be guided to more freedom. I know that is what continues to happen for me. Trust that it will happen for you and your loved ones.

My sister has strong visual memories; I don't, and we have an agreement that this is by design. She remembers visually because she can handle that. I can't look closely at my visual memories. I can have only a few flashes of my dad coming at me. That's enough. I don't need any more. My entire body screams of what I survived. That's how powerful cellular memory is — *the body remembers everything!*

People need to know that it comes up differently for different people. Healing is possible for everyone. I can't say it enough: it's never too late to heal. If we can give ourselves the gifts of healing and sharing our truths, there is so much more on the other side of that — more of ourselves, our essences, our passions, and our power.

FALLING APART COMES FIRST

My life had to completely fall apart before I could make sense out of it and put the pieces back together.

I share about this because we live in a society and culture that teaches us that if something is falling apart, there's no hope: it's to be disregarded and discarded. In some ways, it's true that everything that fell apart for me — my idea of who I was, my idea of my strengths, my idea of what is acceptable — needed to fall apart so that the truth could rise. That doesn't mean the structures didn't serve; they did serve. They served to *keep me together* for all these years. It's the transforming power of falling apart and having the faith that something new will emerge that needs to be shared in our culture. It's the ultimate rebirth.

I didn't know my truth. I didn't know that one of my deepest core beliefs was that I was unlovable and a complete waste of space. I carried that tonality along with extreme sadness and extreme rage.

For years, I made sense of those two oversized feelings by thinking: *Well, I grew up lower-middle class, marginalized, and I was transgender before the word even existed.*

I tried to make sense of my life with those beliefs. Memories of the financial struggles in my family of origin, for example, would awaken only small doses of those feelings of rage and sadness.

When I first got to rehab, I thought that if I started crying, I'd never stop. I thought it would be the same if I started to rage. In the history of humankind, that hasn't happened yet. There's no wailing woman who's been crying nonstop for fifty years. Likewise, there's no raging man holed up in a room with soundproof walls in a museum that you pay ten dollars to visit. Still, I was so afraid of my feelings. We do, however, have to *feel it* to *heal it*.

I've always been an introspective person. I've always been a hugely feeling person. I wasn't in denial. All of this suggests how powerful dissociative thinking is and the split that happens especially when babies and toddlers are abused. They are feeling as though it's a life-or-death situation, and to them it is. They can't even crawl away yet.

I couldn't run away, walk away, crawl away, or speak up. I say all of this because the amount of rage and sadness I carried finally made sense.

The Body's Trauma Response

My body's trauma response was to disconnect, dissociate, and to split. From early on, I didn't think it was safe to have a body, specifically my body, that had been sexually violated. There was a split between my head and my torso. A human can split in so many different ways. I was just a head carrying around a body.

I was shut off sexually and was not able to feel my genitals. I could feel them to some extent, but not with the amount of sensation that I've witnessed other people experiencing. What was going on here?

By my mid-thirties, I had three different experiences that all elicited the same response in me, a physical organism.

One occurred when I was standing in front of an acting class. My teacher told me to pick a person from my life, create the reality that they were sitting in front of me in a chair, and I chose my mom.

The teacher said, "All you have to do is stand very freely and let that person send you nothing but love."

I tried to let that happen. Suddenly I crumpled over, and I was on the floor curled in a fetal position, sobbing.

What the fuck happened?

Another response happened in art school when I was up all night and then watching Sally Jessy Raphael in the morning. Roseanne Barr was on the show. She started talking about her stepfather who had abused her, who had raped her. They didn't use the word *rape* at that time. She was talking about the violation. Next thing I know, I'm crumpled over, and there is a feeling as if my soul is being kicked. It was the same feeling I had when trying to imagine my mom in my acting class. I was on the floor sobbing.

At the time, I thought that my reaction in the acting class was weird. I thought that it was because I hadn't let my mom's love in. But this time, with the words and example of Roseanne Barr, I thought it was because I was so sensitive to her pain. I never made a connection to what had happened to me in childhood. I never had the wherewithal to ask the question.

The third time, I was with one of my best friends, Sirena, for the first time in Los Angeles. We were staying at her friend's Hollywood Hills mansion. We were drinking and had plans to go out dancing later.

She said to me, "Let me just dress you up in my friend's clothes."

I asked, "Her girly clothes?"

She said, "Yeah, it would be fun."

I thought: *Okay, I love Sirena. She's safe. I'm an artist. I can do anything once.*

I let her dress me up. She had me turned away from the mirror so I couldn't see. She put me in a mini skirt, a halter top, things I had never worn, and would never wear in real life. She fixed my hair and makeup, and then she put me in some crazy high-heeled shoes that I could barely put on.

She turned me around on the swivel stool to face the mirror, and I was completely shocked. The person in the mirror was beautiful. In that instant there was a disconnect.

I thought: *How can that person be so beautiful, and yet it's me?*

Instead of thinking: *that's me*, I was thinking *that person.*

That woman was the sort who I'd chase around a club, trying to get her number. How could that be me? This was a completely weird feeling.

Sirena said, "Of course you feel that way. You don't connect to being a beautiful woman, and yet you really are."

She swiveled me back around and asked, "Do you want to try walking?"

She held out her hand so that I could walk in the high heels.

I said, "I don't know if I can walk in these."

I stood up. I trusted her implicitly, which is why I could do this. I stood up, I took maybe three steps in, and I crumpled on the floor sobbing. I had the terrible feeling of being pummeled in my solar plexus.

Neither of us knew what was going on, but Sirena loved me enough and knew enough about caring for people to get down on the ground and hold me and rock me. She held me close. She rocked me sweetly. I sobbed like I'd never sobbed before with another human being.

I wasn't trying to make excuses or figure out why this occurred. I didn't have the ability to deflect with humor. This was an all encompassing emotional release like I'd never experienced before. It was huge. It scared both of us.

I didn't understand what this was about. This was the third time I had collapsed or crumbled with these intense feelings. I told her the stories. She didn't know, either. She continued to hold me, rocking me gently, as a mother would a child.

I still didn't have the wherewithal to say: *What the fuck happened to me?*

In hindsight years later, when I was looking at this from a different perspective in therapy, of course I could finally ask, "What the fuck happened to me?"

Trusting the Process

I had to learn to trust the process even though I was the most scared I'd ever been.

I've already mentioned I got the three-year restraining order. I'd never had legal problems like that ever, so that was pretty huge. And then making the choice to smoke crack for a year and three months was a visceral choice, the choice of the body and the mind to escape. But my higher self knew it wasn't a great choice, in fact, it was a dangerous choice. I really didn't care. Even having that information, I was choosing danger and isolation. That was all part of my life falling apart. For my fellow obsessive-compulsive disorder (OCD) peeps who counted how many times I used the word *choice* in this paragraph, just know that you're not alone.

The biggest challenge was when I finally had to go to rehab and trust that I couldn't do it alone. I couldn't fix my life by myself. I needed help. I needed a container and a twenty-four/seven safety environment that I could only find with an inpatient residential program.

Getting treatment would be the first time I was going to have to trust that it was safe to ask for and receive help. As a trauma survivor, I learned early on to do everything by and for myself. Asking for help often equated asking for trouble.

I remember getting to treatment and crying, being so grateful and so scared at the same time, saying, "Thank you for helping me," and just sobbing.

I knew that I had to let it all fall apart. I had to let all the tears fall and the ideas and social constructs fall to figure out what my essence was and build up from that.

Family Members Come Forward — I Was Not Alone

First and foremost, I want to share about my sister, who came forward saying that she thought for years that she was the pervert, she was the freak. Almost every night she would have nightmares about our dad. It was always him sexually violating her.

She always thought, as many people do: *My dad wouldn't do that to me. I must be the sick one.*

If a victim doesn't have cognitive memory, and if the memory is only in a deeper level of consciousness or on a cellular level, and it only comes up in dreams or flashbacks, they often think that they themselves are the disturbed one to have thoughts like that.

When I came forward with my story, my sister was able to come forward and share hers and get herself into recovery. She's done a ton of healing and is working a rock-solid program of recovery. I'm so proud of her.

My solo show, *Learning to Stay*, which is specifically about my abuse, addiction and healing, is available online. My aunt, who I'd been estranged from, watched it and contacted me. She said that she, too, had a story about my dad. When she was four and he was fourteen, he sexually abused her. This was back in the 1950s. In the clearest language that she could summon at the time, she told on him. Thank God my grandparents listened, and they took him to a psychiatrist.

The story we always heard as a family was that they thought he was gay, so they sent him to an all-boys military school in Georgia. The real story was that they thought he was a danger to the two girls in the family, so they sent him away.

Hearing my aunt's story marked the first time in my life, and I was about forty-one years old, that I didn't feel crazy. I already had my sister telling me the same stories about my dad. But it helped to have one other person verify it. This was meaningful for my sister, too, and helped us heal more deeply.

CHAPTER THREE

Humor as a Life Saver

CLASS CLOWN

I was happy taking on the role of class clown as early as I can remember.

One of the reasons I'm on this planet is to remind people to play. I love connecting with and bringing joy to people. Nothing makes me happier than making people laugh. Especially when I use body language and physical humor, because that's the only language we share. There's nothing quite like crossing a language barrier. It's a direct connection from heart to heart. It's an instant up-leveling of vibration and frequency and overall being-ness. People feel better when they're laughing.

I used to work for a catering company in northern California. There was a Chinese woman who had been working there for eons. She spoke very little English. She was not interested in learning it, either. She got her work done just fine. I'd make her laugh to the point of tears and crossing her legs to keep from peeing. It was physical comedy. She would be working and very serious, maybe she would be behind schedule, and I'd drop to all fours and crawl across the kitchen floor in front of her until she cracked up.

So many people think that at a certain age, you have to stop playing.

They say, "What are you doing?" and "Who do you think you are?" and "Act your age!"

We all have a child in us who needs and wants to play. Play is such a high form of expression.

Flirting With the Girls

Who doesn't like someone who's funny and charming?

Girls are easy to flirt with when you use humor. When I was young, I'd get nervous and excited around certain cute girls. Making a joke was the easiest and most fun way to light them up and make them happy and, most important, make them remember me.

I knew I wasn't a boy by birth, even though I knew I was a boy. In fourth grade, my sense of humor was kicked up a notch because it was a way to flirt without being overtly flirtatious; it was my way to make people feel good. I clearly loved making cute girls laugh.

As I mentioned before, I had a super crush on one girl. I was in third grade, and she was in first grade, and my crush lasted for many years. In the beginning, there were times when I'd get up early on school days and make a gift for her. I'd make little cards or arts and crafts, hearts, and so on. I just needed her to know that she was the love of my life nine years into it.

I remember asking my sister, Susan, who was also in first grade, "Would you please give this to Kathryn Washington?"

Finally, after many school days and many random gifts, Susan said, "You give it to her yourself!"

I think Kathryn and I were together in a past life. To this day, I've such a sweet spot for her in my heart, and I don't really even know her. I could definitely make her laugh. That was one thing I had going for me.

The Principal's Office

I was in the principal's office a few times in middle school, but I don't remember exactly why. However, I do remember the reasons I was sent to the principal in high school.

Later in high school I acted out a creative fuck-you on the school. Keywords: *acted out*. It was around Easter.

I hard-boiled about six dozen eggs, dyed them, and wrote on each one:

REDEEM AT OFFICE FOR PRIZE

I put up elaborate homemade posters that stated:

SCHOOLWIDE EASTER EGG HUNT TODAY!

I put the posters up when all the kids were at lunch. I got such pleasure out of stepping back and watching all the students swarm to the office with the eggs they found. My locker was right across from the office, and I watched the two elderly office ladies.

I could only imagine what they were saying to one another: "Mildred, did you know nothin' 'bout some school-wide Easter egg hunt today, don't it?"

They were baffled. The kids all left the office feeling dejected and overwhelmed. Those posters looked legitimate. I've found that if a poster looks legitimate, people think the event has to be real.

No one got hurt. It was a roundabout way of saying *Welcome to my world.* Welcome to the confusion, loneliness, and weirdness of my existence.

Those are the times I got in trouble. I talked my way out of the first one, and in the second case, I surrendered. I got in trouble because a broken egg got into the carpet. It's one of my favorite stories because it was a weird unifier; it was not a mean unifier. I was simply acting out as a teenager. I was transgender, horny as hell, and didn't know how to flirt with or approach girls. Nobody was talking about LGBTQ issues at the time. Nobody else I knew was LGBTQ. I did have one gay friend in school, who was two years younger, my sister's age. Thank God we had each other.

PRANKS, PLAYFULNESS, AND CONNECTION WITH OTHERS

We all have access to our playful nature. Even if growing up you weren't allowed or encouraged to play, there's still an innate desire to play. We can see this in the animals all around us, whether they are pets or in the wild. Play happens naturally.

What I know to be true is that when people play, there's an ease of connection and many defenses fall away. If people can let themselves know it's safe enough to play, there's an expansiveness that takes place. It's a deeply spiritual thing to be connected to life itself and one another through laughter and a lightness of being.

I know from my experience that playfulness is a great way to create bridges and disarm people, whether it's a friendly joke or a friendly comment on a shared experience. Taking people out of their own paradigm and into a shared paradigm is healing for all of us.

Making People Laugh

Making people laugh is the biggest high I know. I've done a lot of drugs, and I've also been a stand-up comic, and there's no drug like stand-up when it works. When stand-up works, especially when I'm doing my material and allowing myself to improv and work with what's in the room at the present time, there's no high like it. Especially when the audience trusts you enough to collectively take that trip with you — nothing compares.

On the flip side, there's nothing like it when it *doesn't* work. That is a very lonely place. I've been there a few more times than I've wanted to be.

One thing I love is being able to go across the cultural divide of language and bring people out of their shells, when they don't speak the language and even are scared to laugh.

Comedy helps people out of their stress and misery. I don't think most people are miserable, but I do think a lot of us tend to dwell on what coulda been, shoulda been, woulda been. It's wonderful to bring people back into present time with something completely abstract and love-based.

My body is my instrument. My work, love, and my art, all involve working with and through my body. Being transgender, and not feeling at home in my body for most of my life, has — needless to say — been a huge challenge. Deciding to transition has given me more freedom in my expression, especially in performance. I recently did stand-up for the first time as *Quinn*. I hadn't done a comedy set in about twelve years. It was a completely new experience to be in the right body and telling my truth.

Pranks

In the early 1990s, I bought a pair of men's Levi's with a size sixty-five waist, which is pretty huge. They are huge and hard to find. I bought them knowing I'd get some laughs out of them some day.

When I was at rehearsal at a friend's home, I'd excuse myself, use the bathroom, and bring said pants out of my backpack and gently drape them over the shower curtain. I'd do this close to the end of rehearsal and just leave.

I'd be giggling all the way home. After all, real men giggle.

I'd wait for the phone call: "What the fuck? Where did you find these? It *was* you, right?"

It doesn't even matter if someone thinks it's funny or not. I can crack myself up just imagining my friends walking into the bathroom and seeing those huge Levi's. Just imagining it brings me so much joy.

When my dear friend Susan and her husband, Jim, lived out in Berkeley, we'd rehearse at their house. They lived like two sloppy bachelors. There was stuff everywhere.

I started taking items from my art pile, or my thrift shop pile, and my trash—that's not quite trash—pile and leaving them in different drawers and cupboards; I wanted to see how long it would take them to notice.

I think it took three or four weeks before Jim said to Susan, "Babe, what the fuck's up with all this crap?"

She said, "Oh, Honey, I thought it was yours."

I thought this was hilarious.

As my mom would say, "It was good, clean fun."

Simple directions to the reader: Go out and have fun with one another. Go out and create some mischief in a healthy way.

PLAY AND PRAYER HAVE THE SAME VIBRATION

I think it's interesting that at this present time on planet Earth, more people regard themselves as *spiritual* rather than *religious*.

As Michael Bernard Beckwith has said, "The vibrations of play and prayer are the same; they both involve touching Reality without trying to get anything from it."

I have lived that fact. Both play and prayer take me outside of my thinking mind, and both take me outside of my situation, my current *isms*. Play brings me to a higher connectedness to myself, to others, and to life itself. Without humor, I know for a fact that I wouldn't be on the planet.

As someone who deals with treatment-resistant severe depression, PTSD, bipolar I, gender dysphoria, and multiple addictions, humor has been a life-saver.

Because my body temple has been riddled with trauma, sadness, and despair, I often wonder: *Which is greater – do I have more sorrow or joy?*

I'm happy to report that even on days where it feels like joy is less, overall I think I've had more joy in my life. To this day, I'm still an optimist. That is a miracle.

Reverend Doctor Michael Bernard Beckwith and His Teachings

I've been a member of Agape going on twenty years. The past ten years I've been following Michael online. Agape offers free live-streaming services twice a week.

These have been instrumental in my staying connected to the message of hope and love and ultimately, a world that works for everyone.

I love what he teaches. I love that he gently pushes the status quo, trusting that we're all in this together and everything is an expression of God. Especially on the days I don't believe that, when I've watched too much of the daily so-called news, I remember the truth of these teachings.

There's rarely been a time when I've attended Agape—in person or at a revelation conference or streamed online—when I didn't feel connected. Maybe once or twice when I was going through a severe depression, I tried to tune in to the service but just couldn't. I was at such a low frequency, such a low vibration, that it seemed that Michael was talking too fast. The music was too loud.

For the most part, when I tune in I feel instantly connected to life, to humanity, to possibility, and to purpose.

What better gift can someone give you?

Thank you, Michael Bernard Beckwith.

Being a *Manny*

I've been a nanny twice in my life, but now I'd call it a *manny*. Once in Boston, I was manny for two little boys, ages two and four. Later, when I got out of LHC in Santa Fe, I was manny for three little boys ages five, six, and seven. The universe kept sending me boys. This not only led me to integrate my own inner boy, but also solidified the reality that we're all spiritual beings having a human experience.

Being around boy energy is pretty incredible. After coming out of treatment, it was great to be with three little guys who were pure energy and a lot of love. Getting down on the floor and playing with them helped me, on some level, to become more integrated and remember more happy moments from my childhood.

We had so much fun. I'm great with kids, and I can quickly find out what makes them laugh. Children aren't in any kind of hurry to hide who they are until they're taught to do so by society. If you're like me, laughing with kids takes you to another level.

Connecting with babies has an added layer of richness. There's no greater prayer than connecting and laughing with a baby. It's almost as if you're laughing with pure source energy.

Laughter elevates one's being in terms of the frequency and vibratory nature. It usually creates or increases a happy state within the person. It's also a full-on internal massage for the body. Modern science is proving not only how good meditation is for us, but also that humor heals.

I've had so many people thank me for my humor and for being so free and weird with it.

I'll take that.

The Healing Benefits of Laughter

There are many people who have healed themselves with laughter. There are people diagnosed with terminal cancers who watched comedic movies, stand-up comedy, and good-feeling comedy that doesn't put people down and were healed. People can heal themselves with laughter and the endorphins that are released as a result. Laughter can be used along with a healthy diet and other methods. Laughter yoga is a popular phenomenon.

I know for myself and for others that laughter works. For example, the late Dr. Masaru Emoto put water from the same source into different containers, and then printed out words to place on each jar. He used the word pairs like *hate* and *joy*, or *anger* and *laughter*. After imprinting the water with the feelings through speech, he photographed the frozen crystals of both jars of water. The crystals imprinted with *hate* are chaotic and malformed. They don't have any patterns. By contrast, the *joy* and *laughter* crystals are symmetrical and beautiful.

If this experiment doesn't speak volumes about positivity and intention, then what does?

What's the percentage of the human body that is water? I think it's 70 percent or more, a huge reminder that we need to be extra aware about the labels and vibrations we take on. If and when you find yourself dealing with negative self-talk, it's imperative that you change the language, ASAP.

If you're struggling to find time in your life to meditate and pray, try to get outdoors and play and consider it done. That doesn't mean you shouldn't get back to prayer and meditation, but play will help you access that same dimension and frequency.

Simple directions to the reader: play it forward by simply playing more!

CHAPTER FOUR

From Surviving to Thriving

MOUSING AROUND ON THE PLANET

I'm sharing this because it's important for everyone to know they can change their state of being, and that includes changing their sense of themselves. As a survivor of childhood sexual abuse, my energetic being was squashed.

I learned early on:

- To be small
- To be invisible
- To be silent

If I was seen or heard, I'd get into more trouble. I couldn't successfully draw attention to the abuse that was happening. Whenever I tried, I was reprimanded for acting out.

I learned early on to see and not be seen. If I'm in a party situation, I scan the party. I know where the exits are, just for safety. Then I scan the faces to know who's there, who's safe, and who isn't. Thankfully, I don't do this as much anymore. I call it *mousing* around the planet. A mouse can mouse around the planet, and that's fine, it fits their size. But no human adult should be mousing around.

"Your Apology Gift Is in the Mail"

There were times in my life where I felt so much shame for who I was as a body and as a story. I was over-identified with the story of my life. I didn't know that I could separate the two. I thanked people profusely for simply meeting me. Or, at least, that's the energy I brought forward. There was a sense of reverse desperation, if there can be such a thing.

I'd joke, saying, "Your apology gift is in the mail," because before you even met me, I was so sorry you were going to. I never sent those gifts, but I carried that vibration.

When I mention this to people who know me well, they get it. I don't have to carry that energy anymore. On that note, I was always the one who came bearing gifts. If I were to show up without a present of some sort, that just wasn't enough. That has shifted, too. I am finally learning that I am enough.

Disempowerment Versus Empowerment

I was more comfortable for most of my life giving my power away. I believe that if I gave it to someone else, I wouldn't be left holding the power. I had such a skewed vision of people with power. People with power abuse it. There was abuse in my family, and you can turn on the news and see abuse of power, whether it's politics or police brutality. I had a weird sense. I didn't know it was okay to be powerful. I thought if I was powerful, I'd be an abuser.

Even in work situations, when bosses wanted to promote me, I cringed at the thought. I didn't want any stature in the work hierarchy. I didn't want to be a part of that at all. I learned that every time I gave my power away, a little tiny part of me died, or was decreased. I've been rebuilding that power over the past years, figuring out what authentic power is and what power without ego is. It's a work in progress

Taking Full Responsibility for My Life

Knowing that I'm the author of my life, do I want to be writing a tragedy, a comedy, or a romance?

It should be a healthy mix of all those things, so I'm not lopsided and not living on only one end of the spectrum of human emotion. As I write this, I'm a little over a year into my new recovery.

Most days have been fairly easy.

The past few days have been very difficult:

- I wanted to drink.
- I wanted to do drugs.
- I wanted to watch porn.
- I wanted to have anonymous sex.
- I wanted to escape my feelings.

I didn't do any of the above. Instead, I sat with all the discomfort and emotional pain.

I also deal with suicidal ideations, and I've had them most of my life. Life is often too overwhelming, too big, too much, and I don't know how to plug into it and be a part of it. Some part of me, and it's the part of me that has PTSD, wants to go away. Escapism by way of one of my multiple addictions is always tempting. The ultimate escape would be to take my own life.

I've made a commitment *not* to do that. I will continue to learn to stay.

I made a contract with people who love me:

- My girlfriend
- My mom
- My sister
- My niece
- My therapist

- My best friends
- My sponsor

The contract simply says that I won't kill myself. If I feel like I'm a danger to myself or others, I've made a commitment to go the ER. Some days it's really hard to figure out how to stay on this planet and be as sensitive as I am. I don't feel like I'm broken. Rather, I just have such a hard time doing what other people seemingly do with ease.

Note to self: quit comparing. If you insist upon comparing, you're only allowed to compare yourself to your former self.

Right here, right now, I'm doing that, one day at a time, often one hour at a time, one minute at a time, knowing that if I don't stay clean and sober, I can't have the life of my dreams. I have to do the inner work, which feels daunting at times. I have to keep going. I have to keep investigating the inner workings of my life. I have to commit to my spiritual connection. That's the only way toward a life worth living.

There's a quote from Socrates, "The unexamined life is not worth living," which implies that if you don't understand your inner world, you should wonder what you are doing.

I've been looking inward a long time; now I need to look outward.

Dear Reader,

If you are a mouse, and you are mousing around the planet, you're doing great.

Every other sentient being: step up and into who you are.

A MORE CONSISTENT WAY OF BEING

I'm hoping that a new, consistent way of being will become more solidified for myself and for anyone reading this who wants it. I've been diagnosed with bipolar I, which is the most intense type. Extreme ups and downs have been the story of my life. Dealing with both manic and severe depressive episodes is nothing to joke about. However, I'm not the diagnoses or labels given to me. I choose to transcend them.

Whenever I'm speaking about my mental illness as it's defined in the *Diagnostic and Statistical Manual* (DSM-V), I speak about *lack of mental wellness at this moment*, to show that it's changeable, and I'm not stuck in that mental state. It's a pretty daunting list of things I'm working with and around daily, whether it's the recovery from multiple addictions, PTSD, bipolar I, suicidal ideations, or the transgender piece. It's a lot to wake up to every morning. Not every single day's a huge struggle, but there are still too many that seem impossible to face.

I insist upon being transparent about this because the more we talk about it, the more as a culture we name it, claim it, identify it, and the less we have to be it. If we name it and claim it, it doesn't have to have power over us.

These aha moments are for me, too. I don't like the sense of separation that comes from saying *you, you, you*. Instead let's say *we, we, we*.

There is a saying in recovery: There is an *I* in illness, and a *we* in wellness. Let's get well together.

Fear

I've heard that there are only two frequencies in the world: love and fear. Everything else is an offshoot or by-product of these two. Actually, there is only love, the absence of which is fear. I can experience love and so much joy, and on the flip side, I can experience fear, and the overwhelming sadness and paralysis that accompany it. It's the exact opposite to the love and the expansion. I feel fear, and I contract and shut down. I've lived a huge portion of my life in that way.

As I was sharing earlier, if sleep were a bank, I could give everybody hours and hours and hours of sleep. I had a friend in college whom I visited perhaps five or six years after graduation.

She said, "You don't remember because you slept through the whole semester."

I said, "What?"

She said, "Yeah, you slept that whole semester."

I go, "No one can sleep through a whole semester."

She said, "Well, you did."

This was before I was even doing hard drugs. I was just checked out. It was easier and safer for me to stay in bed than to be in the world.

I'm doing my best day to day not to go to sleep and check out, but having said that, right here, right now is my first day out of bed in six days.

I'm hiding from something, but what is it?

I'm hiding from fear and being overwhelmed and depression and all the ensuing snowballing events that follow. Fear is a thing. Fear is real. We all must find ways that work for each of us to pull ourselves back into the love vibration—the truth of life.

A newborn baby doesn't feel afraid. Nature isn't shaking in fear. Fear happens in moments. But those of us with PTSD and traumatic events in our lives need to clear the trauma because the body holds onto it. If we aren't doing the work to clear our cells of trauma, it can rear its ugly head and trip us up. I've been working my ass off, but obviously, there's a lot more work to do.

When you're scared, you may realize that you're in *fear*, so break it down:

- **False Evidence Appearing Real:** Check the facts. Are you responding to what only appears to be? Do the investigative work to see what's underneath. Are you projecting or in transference? If so, then you're probably not able to clearly see reality.

- **Fuck Everything and Run:** This is self-explanatory. Seriously, you still have questions? Refer back to earlier in the book, the subheading called "Geographic Stress."

- **Face Everything and Recover:** This is the ultimate gift you can give yourself. This is for addicts and non-addicts alike. Breathing into reality and the knowing that life is on purpose. When it seems overwhelming, you break it down into incremental pieces that you're comfortable with. Just focus on doing the next right thing.

I don't know about you, but I'm choosing the third and final option.

The Grey Area

During most of my twenties, I wore only black and white clothing. That's it. Black and white.

How extreme and interesting a fashion statement is that?

I convinced myself that I didn't look good in any other color. I can laugh at that now. I have one photo in particular that shows my fashion sense.

In this photo, I'm exhausted. I'm not in my element. I'm overworked, underpaid, and not happy — wearing black and white.

I'm laughing now because I'm really trying to be in the grey area. I'm getting better. I know there has to be a kinder, gentler way. I'm still pulled back and forth by black-and-white, all-or-nothing thinking, by a culture that says, *Bigger, faster, famous, yesterday*, as if it's an all-exciting ride. I think that on one level we're all exhausted because we're on a human hamster wheel, otherwise known as a *humanster wheel*—I just made that up— going nowhere, thinking we're almost there. If and when we finally get there, we find out we're two days late. It's no wonder both disappointment and expectation are such painful topics.

Are you trying to get real about what life is about?

At the end of the day, in the middle of the day, in the beginning of the day, throughout the day, when we check in, all we're supposed to be doing—according to Abraham Hicks and other spiritual teachers—is creating more joy for ourselves, to be in the joy, to be in the vibration of joy, helping to heal ourselves and the planet. I definitely have moments of joy, but I haven't been able to sustain it the way I'd like to.

Choosing Life

April 12, 2006, was the day I was finally able to put the crack pipe down and board a plane from Los Angeles to Santa Fe to go to the Life Healing Center. I had missed two flights on two previous days because I couldn't get out of the hotel room and put the pipe down. That day is set in my memory because it was one of the first times as an adult—I was thirty-eight then—that I was asking for help. It was ingrained in me as a survivor of sexual abuse that it's not safe to ask for help. If you have to ask for help, you have to be very careful about whom you ask.

I was at a point in my life where I had to trust that somebody outside of myself could help me. I'll never forget that flight. Even while in the air, I still had reservations about whether it was safe. I had smoked crack every day for a year and three months, trying to die. I was down to 120 pounds.

I remember sitting on the airplane watching the pulse in the vein on my wrist go slower and slower and slower as I was holding my breath. That's how scared I was to get help outside of myself. But I knew I couldn't do it. That's why I thought I'd hold my breath and kill myself on the plane. *Southwest Flight 412, we have a dead person.* I don't know if anyone has ever died from holding their breath. I was thinking: *I will be the person that does it.*

I'll never forget arriving on the property that night. I was crying uncontrollably, thanking everyone for helping me. Snot everywhere, crying from such a wounded-toddler place — I had cried from that place before, but never at this depth. That's when I knew I had to choose life. I wasn't supposed to die. I'd touched death a couple of times in my drug using with at least one or two seizures. One experience was particularly scary. When I arrived at the Life Healing Center I chose life, and I've been working toward reclaiming it ever since.

Soon, I'll have eleven years off crack cocaine. That doesn't mean I haven't dabbled in other things that have gotten me in trouble.

When you're new in recovery, they encourage you to go to ninety meetings in ninety days. What was daunting was getting up and out of bed, getting dressed, and going out into the world ninety days in a row. I couldn't remember the last time I'd done that. Doing that was a bit of a wake-up call.

IT'S SAFE TO BE IN YOUR BODY

It's safe to not only have a body but to be experienced in it.

The biggest challenge for me and the best gift I can give myself is to reclaim safety in my body and enjoy my life. I've spent most of my life not connected to my body. There are so many ways you can split, whether you're separating your head from your torso or splitting right down the middle or left and right or above and below the waist. These splits happen because of trauma, specifically sexual trauma.

I spent most of my life being split, head and body. My head was present. I'm very cerebral. I'm funny and clever. The body can be present, but it's secondary: it communicates after the head.

The more I allow myself to be fully embodied — mind, body, and spirit — the more I come into alignment with mind and body around the transgender piece, the further I'm into my transitioning, the more all of this makes sense. It's incredible what can happen in terms of circuitry. But when I'm connected and in alignment, I light up differently, and I can light others up differently and encourage them to become more embodied.

I've Been Homeless My Whole Life

I've been homeless my whole life because I wasn't at home in my body.

For years, I thought that I felt homeless because my father moved the family so often for his military career. Later I learned that I had never landed where I was moved to. I never really felt comfortable where I was because I never felt comfortable where I was in my body. I was not in the process of knowing that could even happen.

The earliest I remember researching gender reassignment surgery was when I was eighteen years old in my hometown of Fredericksburg, Virginia, scrolling through microfiche files. This was in the late 1980s. There wasn't much to find.

I do remember the few moments I've felt that I was coming home. The first time I ever went to Agape, the building was on Centinela Street near Olympic in a huge warehouse over near the beach in Santa Monica, California. It was a Wednesday night service. There was light music playing. I looked around and saw a few gay couples, a transgender male-to-female, all kinds of people, of all colors and shapes. I sat down as if I were sitting down into myself for the first time ever. I'll never forget that moment.

I thought: *Wow, these are my people. This is diversity. This is love.*

I don't remember my thoughts as much as the feelings. I knew with every part of my being that I was completely safe there. The tears of gratitude began to flow with this soulful homecoming.

My Soul's Choice

I know now that my soul chose my circumstances — I had a soul contract with my dad for the abuse; I agreed to my transgender reality, and the fact that I'd be a performer with the implicit need to be embodied to do my work.

I share this from a place of deep knowingness, not a place of working backwards and wanting to make sense of my life. When I first read the work of Caroline Myss, the author of *Sacred Contracts,* it just made sense. No part of me questioned it. In the same way, I don't question reincarnation. That simply resonates as true.

Embracing these beliefs has me stepping into more and more responsibility. I arrived at that *aha* moment. If I were to dwell on all the stuff that happened to me, I could stay in victim consciousness my whole life. But in saying that I as a soul *chose* these things for my soul's development, I'm able to accept some responsibility. Sometimes that pisses me off, but you know what? That's okay, too. This means the soul is pushing through stuff, growing and moving through things.

I'm struggling to be in my body, and my body is my instrument.

What could be more rich than that?

There's the potential for conflict resolution in every given moment of my life.

I think this holds true for everybody. If we really do the deeper work, we find that our biggest challenges lead us to our gifts and talents.

My Body Is My Vehicle and My Instrument

Early on, I knew I loved theater, but I didn't want to play a girl. The earliest shows I remember doing in kids' theater included a skit based on *Goldilocks and the Three Bears*, and I was Papa Bear. It thrilled me to no end to go shopping and get Papa Bear clothes. It was just boys' brown pants and a brown long-sleeved shirt. We went right to the boys' section, which was where I always wanted to shop anyway.

I played male characters all through high school. In a one-act play festival, I played a guy, and the judges didn't even know I was born female, so they didn't make special note of it. I took that as a huge accolade. There was nothing better than being accepted as a boy, which matched exactly how I felt.

As an actor, I didn't want to be sent out for roles in which I played the girl who lives down the hall. It was so weird when I was in Los Angeles those ten years and trying to figure out how to break into commercial acting. It really wasn't happening, and it wasn't supposed to.

I chose instead to focus on stand-up, sketch, and improv comedy. These are the areas in which I can shine because I can be anybody. I can play a goofy female character without having to put a skirt on. I later found my true calling: one-person shows. In them, I can tell my full truth all the time.

I recently was signed by an agent in Albuquerque and Los Angeles. She pitched me for a role of a female-to-male character.

My first thought was a negative one: *This is probably a project that won't come to life. This film probably won't get funding. Blah, blah, bickety-blah.*

Then I looked the project up online and found out that it's a TV show that's been running for three years. Only then did I get excited about the idea of being on an episode.

I had to fill out my information online on an Actors' Access website I hadn't even heard of before. I hadn't filled out these kinds of forms in twenty years, and I'd never worked with an agent before.

I could self-sabotage at any minute, thinking: *What if I can't do it?*

I input my new full name: Quinn Alexander Fontaine. This was also the first form on which I checked *male*. I was pretty psyched! This was the new me.

Later I wondered: *Why don't they have a box for trans? I'm not going to go out on any auditions for buff dudes.*

That brought up another layer of self-acceptance, working with the body I'm in, pushing forward, and making a way for myself in the world.

CHAPTER FIVE

Being a Beneficial Presence on the Planet

CHOOSING TO HELP EVERYWHERE I GO

I've grown from not wanting to be on the planet to choosing to help whenever I can. I want to talk about this because to this day I still have suicidal ideations. I continue to deal with thoughts of self-sabotage that tell me I don't deserve to take up space on the planet.

Why am I here?

What's the meaning of life?

Many of us have these existential questions. They can arise even if a person isn't suicidal and doesn't go to that level in their thinking in terms of not knowing how to be here on Earth, and not knowing what to do with their lives.

You have the power to turn that thinking around. Just as much as you may feel unplugged — unable to grab onto life, feel, and be passionate about it — there's the flip side where you can completely enjoy your life. I know this to be true because I've experienced it for myself.

I encourage you to find out what lights you up. What lights you up from the inside out? That's the key to being a beneficial presence on the planet, being more plugged in, more connected, more inspired, and more uplifted. The more all of us are of those things, we can give that gift to others to keep us shining our light. That is pretty magical.

The Pivotal Time to Choose Life and Recovery

When I was finally able to put the crack pipe down in Los Angeles, I parked my car at the long-term parking lot, idealistically thinking I wouldn't be gone that long, and flew to New Mexico for treatment. I thought I'd be there for thirty days at the most.

Walking away from that crack pipe was like leaving a lover I knew I needed to leave. A lover who didn't love me back. Choosing that lover was choosing death, slowly but surely. Each step I took toward the terminal gate, getting on the plane, each mile toward Santa Fe—to the place I was going to get my life back—was not only a conscious decision to save my life, but also a choice to believe that it had to finally be safe to ask for help.

The inability to ask for help stemmed from my early childhood trauma. I finally surrendered to letting people help me and see me in my vulnerability. When you choose to be vulnerable and real, you are choosing to be your strongest. That was the first time I remember actively choosing life.

Feeling Your Power and Feeling Your Purpose

I've come upon lots of different ways to feel my authentic power.

I chased power in all the superficial ways:

- By using manipulation
- By using speed and other drugs to conquer my own nervous system
- By attaining money and material objects to feel a false sense of power

In the healthy ways that I've found my authentic power, it's a higher high than a drug. And it's also a lower low than a drug. But it's real. And that's what I choose to experience these days. I'm living life on life's terms.

When I first think about this, and I ask myself what is the best thing to share, it has to be my humor. There is so much power in humor. I've made a conscious decision to use my comedy in a proactive, productive, and inspiring way.

I like to get up on stage and present an idea of fun based on the human condition that raises everyone to a higher level. I don't like to point out so-and-so in a certain chair or talk about a certain demographic and be angry, mean, and hateful. I could do that. That would be easy. I choose to take the comedic high road.

In sharing my humor, especially in improv situations in everyday life, I like to pop that bubble of reality and bring others into my sense of fun.

Playing It Forward

My first solo show is called *Learning to Stay*. It's about learning to stay on the planet and not kill myself, learning to stay in my body and not dissociate, learning to stay with my feelings, moment to moment, and not shut down. Expanding on this, I've created the three-step concept for the PLAY IT FORWARD workshop.

1) Learning to Stay
2) Staying to Play
3) Playing it Forward

The workshop is in its gestation period. More will be revealed in time.

BRINGING YOUR GIFTS FORWARD

Everybody has the ability to bring their gifts and talents forward.

First of all, reincarnation is real.

Second of all, as a soul, we choose our incarnation. We not only choose our families, our race, our gender, and our core issues, but we have soul contracts with other people to come in and play out certain dynamics. Ultimately, our experiences are for our soul's growth. I know this to be true. My whole body lights up when I consider this truth.

We come forward onto this planet each time in a different incarnation with a specific set of gifts and talents that only we can share with our fellow time travelers, our fellow humanoids, and other creatures as well, such as our four-legged, furry friends. If we don't release our gifts and talents, parts of us shrivel up and start to die.

If you aren't in touch with your gifts and talents, there are a few questions you can ask yourself:

- *What lights me up from the inside out?*
- *What excites me more than anything else?*
- *What lights me up with a sense of purpose and childlike wonder?*

Between the ages of four and ten, you have pretty much developed your full personality. Freud believed it happened by age five. From then on, you grow and expand and unfold, and you get more in touch with different aspects of yourself. But you are in your full essence as a child.

Ask yourself:

- *Who was I as a child, and what did I love to do?*

- *What was I like throughout my childhood, and what did I love to do before my energy was squashed?*

- *Who was I before I was redirected, before I was told "boys don't do this" or "girls don't do that"?*

- *Who was I when I was lighting up the room, shining, and being bright?*

When you get in touch with your gifts and talents, you find that you are already equipped to express them, to share them, to give them. It's what you need to do to be fully alive. So, I encourage everybody to ask some of those simple questions. If you aren't already in touch with what lights you up in that way, do a little work to find out. You will feel different—more connected and more inspired. This book will finally make sense.

Every Child has Unique Gifts and Talents

Imagine if our culture told every child that they have unique gifts that are needed on this planet. Imagine if this whole world told every child that they have talents that can be brought forth only through them. All anyone needs to do is to be fully themselves. What a gift this would be!

Not only would this encourage each individual child and their family, but it would also ripple out in all directions, encouraging a whole community and ultimately the world itself. There would be so much less self-hate. Maybe this would cut back on all kinds of addiction. It would cut back on self-medication. When people are self-medicating, it's because they are in a great deal of pain. Allowing children to be true to themselves would alleviate a core level of pain.

Imagine if people were taught to be themselves; first, there would be less ridicule. If only we were taught that we need every individual to be a part of the whole culture; we don't all need to be alike. Imagine we are all on a boat. It's a huge boat, but we can stand in only a few places. If we all stand in the same place, the boat is going to tip. The weight won't be evenly distributed because we are not valuing difference.

We can change that at any time. We don't have to bemoan our childhoods.

We can say right here and right now that we are a unique expression of Love. Love can only express as us, through us, for itself, and for its own unfolding.

Love is continually unfolding through all of us. The minute we start to atrophy and stop our own growth, Love gets stuck in that place. At the same time, Love is always summoning us and encouraging us to do the next right thing for our soul's growth.

The Missing Link Is Love and Acceptance

At age forty-nine, I'm still working on loving and accepting myself. It stems from many years of not feeling loved and accepted. I had never been told that I was cute or even easy on the eyes until I went to college. Someone told me that I was *striking*.

I said, "Fuck you, what do you want from me?"

She was taken aback. "What are you talking about? I'm trying to give you a compliment."

Perhaps I received compliments and simply didn't recognize them; perhaps I pushed them away and didn't remember them. But I don't think that's the case. Growing up transgender in rural Virginia, there were no images of others like me—never mind anyone like me who had achieved success in their careers or in their lives. Not only were there no role models, but almost all religions shunned the LGBTQ community as I was growing up. This continues to change. For that, I'm so grateful.

Ultimately, you want to be seen, felt, heard, and loved. You want to know you make a difference. Ultimately everyone needs these simple things.

This need starts in infancy. Studies show that when babies aren't touched, their health declines, and they fail to thrive. Not by coincidence, this is classified as *Failure to Thrive*. The psychoanalysts John Bowlby and Renée Spitz studied children, orphans in World War II. Bowlby went on to form the evolutionary theory of attachment. It states that children are born with the innate need to form physical and emotional attachments with others. This is a built-in survival mechanism. We all need healthy touch.

Even if we aren't being touched physically, our hearts need to be touched. Like I mentioned before, a simple, genuine, heartfelt, authentic smile from one stranger to another can connect, inspire, and uplift. Probably on some level, it can calm the nervous system. I know that in my experience, I've been in a world of panic, and if someone gives me the acknowledgement of a smile, a nod, or a friendly gesture, some part of me settles down, and I feel that maybe it's okay that I'm here.

I encourage all of us to give a smile when we can, to give love and encouragement when we can to family, to coworkers, and to strangers, whenever it feels authentic and natural. Receive a friendly gesture when it comes your way. Life is about both giving and receiving. Look at nature. Look at the four seasons. Look at what happens to plants in the ground. There is a season for everything. The giving and receiving has to happen for each of us as well.

Choice

Ultimately, there are only two choices: love or fear. The absence of love is fear. Many people think that hate is the opposite of the emotion of love. This may be obvious, but underneath hate is always fear. I can have a rage fest, and when I get to the end of my rage, there is always a huge number of tears that need to flow.

Am I choosing love or fear?

If I'm afraid, it means I need to love. We all answer this question for ourselves. Yes, we can get feedback from our friends and families and loved ones and any professionals who are helping us. Ultimately, we get to choose from moment to moment.

Am I choosing love or fear?

When we choose love, life gets softer, kinder, gentler, and much more beautiful.

I know you have probably already heard this, but the reality of one's perception is based on the state of our being. The world looks gloomy, dismal, and frightening when we are gloomy, dismal, and frightened. On the other hand, the world looks beautiful, bright, happy, shiny, and loving when we are beautiful, bright, happy, and so on. I know this for a fact—I've been on both ends of the spectrum—to the *nth* degree. When you feel hateful, spiteful, angry, shut-down, and scared, then this is what the world looks like. When this happens to me, it's a reminder that I need to work on myself and my attitude.

It's an inside job.

I heard that expression many times in early recovery. At the time, I didn't know what the fuck they were talking about.

I thought: *What do you mean? Get a job and steal from inside the store? What do you mean when you say "it's an inside job"?*

It means that it's our responsibility, and it's a stinky reality for a lot of people. They don't want the responsibility. They want to continue to play the blame game. I've played the blame game, but it does not get you anywhere. I can laugh at myself and say a change in perspective is all it took. In spite of negativity, I actually do believe that the universe is friendly.

Are you with me?

Instructions for Play

Take your inner child to a big store like Target or an art store, somewhere where you can get toys or art supplies or materials. Take your inner child shopping. Go buy whatever your inner child is drawn to so that you can start playing a little bit more and get in touch with something that lights you up.

Or go do something you were told you couldn't or shouldn't do. For example, my ex loved art as a kid, but she wasn't allowed to paint because she'd get dirty. To this day, she has never allowed herself to create art, but she is a huge art collector. I always encouraged her to get dirty, put on a smock, get some finger paints, and start small. Make it primal. Do something that an adult shouldn't do. More important, do something that was perhaps taken away from you as a kid, something that was enjoyable and a part of something that lit you up and got you excited.

COMMUNITY CIRCLE

The idea of a community circle makes me smile. It has taken me a long time to get comfortable with having community. I've always loved people, but I never knew how to be with them because I never knew how to be with myself. As I get to be more comfortable being my own, authentic self, I'm finding the people who are members of my tribe — my Tribesters — and who I need in my life to maintain perspective and balance.

Wherever two or more people are gathered, there we have community. A community can be only two people. It can be two thousand or two million. We each get to decide what feels right for us. It doesn't have to be set in stone; it can ebb and flow, and it can change altogether. I think it's incredibly important to surround yourself with people who not only mirror back the truth of you, but also are trying to better themselves, to uplift their lives, and ultimately to be present on the planet.

There's an *I* in Illness and a *We* in Wellness

I learned that phrase in recovery, but I think it applies to everybody, addicts and non-addicts alike. The minute everything is about I, I, I, you're locked in your own island of self. If I catch someone saying *I* too many times, I start counting how many times they repeat this, but it also lets me know about their world perspective.

If they don't break it down and say, *You, you, you* or *We, we, we*, even if they are in the world, they are somewhat isolated.

The real thing to be mindful about is that the *I* in illness is the isolation piece. This is specifically true for addicts. One of the biggest challenges for addicts is that they do tend to isolate, and as a result, the world gets very small.

If your world is tiny for long periods of time, usually fear is underneath this isolation:

- Fear of others
- Fear of going out in the world
- Fear of being seen
- Fear of experiencing something new

The *we* in wellness reminds me of the song *We Are the World*. I love that song from the early 1980s. I first heard it around Christmastime. It was a hopeful and beautiful song about healing the planet. I remember listening to it and crying.

I was only twelve, and I thought: *Wow, we really can do this together. We really can heal the world. We really can come together as one.*

I'm still hopeful that we can heal the planet and realize we are all the same species. We are Earthlings. We can quit all these crazy divisions. Once we realize we are all Earthlings and in this together, something will shift regarding war and famine and all that insanity. It's amazing to me that while I'm speaking this truth right now, I'm in the minority. But I'm still hopeful, and I do believe people's attitude toward the world is shifting.

Also, I encourage people to have a sense of *we*. It can be two people or two hundred or two thousand, whatever feels right. But it always has to have a two in the number. Just kidding.

Community — Your Neighborhood OR the Planet

I can only speak for America and all the places I've lived here in this country. I've traveled abroad. I backpacked around Europe for a while, but I never landed in one place long enough to truly experience it. I know in America there is a real problem — and I've been a part of it — when people don't get to know their neighbors.

In the last two places I lived, I've gotten to know a few neighbors and invited them into my community. They are part of my tribe. It feels good. I'm learning new ways to be with people and have boundaries. Maybe that was what the fear was before: that I didn't know how to have boundaries.

How could I have boundaries with strangers?

Learning about this has been wonderful.

It doesn't matter whether your community is small or is just your neighborhood. Go ahead and learn about your neighbors. Know what's going on next door. If your community wants and needs to be bigger, then let it be bigger, too. The beauty is you get to create your world.

Anybody who knows me can attest to how I love community. I'm the kind of person who talks to everybody everywhere I go. I love bursting that bubble, that veil between people. I'm not talking shock value stuff, not all the time, anyway. I love to play with people and hopefully make them laugh, but that is not always my intention. I just want to connect. Maybe on a deep level, I want to prove to myself that I'm worthy of connection.

Now that I'm over two years into my transition, and I haven't been called a woman in months, there's a whole different level of ease about being with people and being in the right body.

I encourage you to check in and ask yourself what *your* sense of community looks like. Aside from your family of origin, you get to create a family of choice. You have the power to decide who's a vibrational match for you.

Who gets to be in your tribe?

List of Mentors

Whoever you are and wherever you are on your path, there is always someone who came before you whom you can thank.

I must talk about my amazing mom first. After all, she was my first mentor. She modeled how to be loving, open, resilient, and strong. She's been my number-one fan since the day I was born, and it hasn't always been easy for her. I've been one of her biggest challenges and learning curves. She's told me so. I've witnessed her growth in direct relation to her choosing to love me. My journey with multiple addictions, treatment-resistant severe depression, and my transgender reality have taken her on her own journey. I'm honored and proud of all the work she's done to keep her heart open. I love you, Mom!

I definitely give credit to my best friend, Susan, who's loved me through so much. She's been my best friend for over twenty years, and she's my creative partner. The level of fun we have and the depth of our friendship continually amazes me. Susan's one of the best people I know. How lucky am I to have her walking beside me?

Not only that, but she's the mother of four. All four kids used to call me Uncle Kathleen. Now they call me Uncle Quinn. I've been a part of their lives since they were babies.

Next on the list has to be Michael Bernard Beckwith. I've been a member of Agape since the late nineties. Michael's essence stayed the same. He hasn't changed. He's only grown and expanded, lifted up more and more people, and continued to look younger all the while. He doesn't talk about his age; he talks about his spirit, which is timeless. He's given me so many gifts and gently led me back to my true self time and time again.

For you, the reader who doesn't know about Agape, go online and check it out: www.agapelive.com. They stream three live services each week. No matter where you are on the planet, they're making the message available — that we are all one and that Love is the answer.

Right after Michael comes his wife, Rickie Byars-Beckwith. I love her voice, her essence, and her childlike sense of wonder. I love witnessing her in her fullness. She's one of the most talented and embodied souls I know. She's 100 percent real all the time.

The Beckwiths are a huge reason that I'm still on the planet. Even when I feel disconnected, disenfranchised, dis-whatevered, I can tune into Agape and feel connected to hope and life again. Agape reminds me that each of us is *on-purpose with purpose*.

My ex of almost nine years, Debbie, taught me so much by example. She's truly one of the best souls I know and is truly a lover of humanity. She saw things in me that I didn't see in myself. She gave me so many healing opportunities. Debbie gave me so much wisdom. She inspired me to follow my heart and contribute on a deeper level.

I got kicked out of rehab. I went right into suicidal thinking. I had no exit plan for leaving treatment, and I was terrified.

I told the staff at the Life Healing Center, "I need to stay here and make a plan. More important, I need to say goodbye in the community circle."

The circle took place two days later.

"I need to say goodbye because I've been mousing around the planet, not knowing how to communicate directly," I said. "I have to thank everybody here who's helped me."

They heard me loud and clear, and they let me stay. They prescribed drugs to sedate me. I was on suicide watch for those two nights. Someone had to sit with me in the room both nights while I slept.

I showed up with the song I'd chosen to share. When you say goodbye in the community circle, you get to speak to the group and play music of your choice. You can go around the whole circle and ask each person, one-on-one, if it's okay to hug them goodbye. I knew that if I didn't do this, I'd be leaving in a way that wasn't complete.

I did it. I did it, and it ended up being one of the most powerful experiences of my life. I used the song *Thank You for Hearing Me, Thank You for Seeing Me* by Sinead O'Connor. If you haven't heard this song, give yourself the gift of listening to it.

Photos

BABASTÉ! My inner baby sees your inner baby and all is truly well. This is my version of NAMASTÉ. Even though I've identified this age—four to six months old—as the time when my father began to abuse me, I see hope and power in this little guy's face. I love you, baby Quinn!

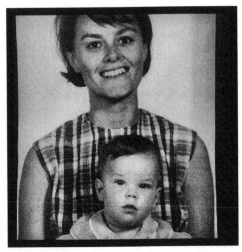

First passport photo. This is me, eleven months after I first met my sweet mom. Is it just my perspective now or is that one intense baby stare-down?

My beautiful mom, Nancy, and me. I was about two years old. I've always loved this photo of us.

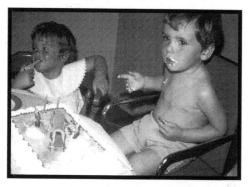

The note on the back of this photo reads "Kathleen Plays Russian Roulette." I've always been amused by this photo.

This is me at six years old: Junior cowboy. My family was on a cross-country trip, and Mom bought me my first cowboy boots, belt, hat, and jeans. I never wanted to take them off.

My sister, Susan, and I before a swim meet. She was nine, and I was eleven. I was already beginning to hunch over to hide my pre-pubescent body.

Me at sixteen, preparing to deliver a stick of butter to my grandma's house. The trench coat and hardhat were my cry for help.

Nude Coffee, an all-female sketch comedy group, circa 1996. Left to right: me, Sirena Irwin, and Susan Mele. *Note: While this book was in the editing phase, Nude Coffee performed in our first two reunion shows after fifteen years of not being on stage together. It was my first show as a trans guy and it was beyond wonderful.* I love these two with all my heart!

Stand-up photo headshot featuring my leg, circa 1998. I wore my hair slicked back in a ponytail for over twenty years. It was the *helmet look.* Safety first!

Wedding dress 1.0 (standing version). This was a fun shoot. The photographer, Wendy York, asked me to bring a spectrum of my wardrobe. I was a twenty-something starving artist and had no wardrobe from which to have a spectrum. I showed up to her studio with an industrial-size carton of aluminum foil, a roll of police caution tape, a pair of black combat boots and a pair of men's black Calvin Klein underwear—boxers, not briefs. She acknowledged my concept of fashion and encouraged me to try on the wedding dress that was hanging nearby. The rest is history/herstory! [Photo by Wendy York]

Wedding dress 2.0 (sitting version). I always felt like a bad drag queen whenever I wore a dress. The wedding dress photos capture that. I see the beauty, but I mostly feel the disconnect. Let's just call it cute and crispy. [Photo by Wendy York]

Crack cocaine chapter of my life. When healing my preverbal childhood sexual abuse became too much, I chose drugs. I smoked crack daily for a year and three months, trying to die. I include this because it's real, and it's the only time I felt comfortable being naked. I weighed an unhealthy 120 pounds.

This is my last professional headshot as Kathleen Fontaine. I'd just been cast as one of the original members of *The Show* in Albuquerque, New Mexico. I almost didn't audition because I thought I was too old. The casting notice said, "Looking for great male and female improvisers ages eighteen to thirty-five." I was forty-four. [Photo by Frank Frost Photography]

Selfie during a psychotic break. I took this self-portrait right before being admitted to Menninger psychiatric hospital. I posted it on my Facebook page because I wanted people to see and know the real deal.

Conclusion

Welcome to the conclusion. If life were only this simple. First, I want to thank you and congratulate you for getting through this book. You, too, are a survivor, and I hope that you're feeling the thriving energy moving through your body. If nothing else, I hope reading this book has made you think, laugh, cry, rethink, re-laugh, and re-cry. Ultimately, the gift I want to give you is the gift of possibility, of knowing that right now, right where you are *is* the perfect time and place to be more *you* than ever before.

You are not your story. Whatever your story may have been before this moment, you as much as I have the power to change the script at any moment, to get more and more in touch with your essence, to be who you truly are. You are always your essence, and you can always choose to be a bigger, brighter, shinier version of your essence. You can choose to shine your light more brightly. That's my message.

Whenever I see someone take the risk or have the courage to be more genuine in whatever's happening at any given moment — whether it be extreme vulnerability or extreme elation, or anywhere in between — whenever I see them being truly themselves, it gives me permission to do the same.

I hope you feel inspired. I hope you're telling other people to pick up this book. It might help and inspire them, too, to be more themselves, if nothing else. If you give yourself the gift of simply that, being true to who you are moment to moment, then unconsciously and without even intending to, that gift ripples out and gives others permission to do the same. Ultimately, I know what the world needs more of: people being authentic and heart-based from moment to moment.

Anytime I say to myself in frustration: *I have to figure this out*, I catch myself and say: *No. I need to feel my way through or into this.*

It's a feeling reality. We are emotional creatures all the time.

That's one thing I learned from Eve Ensler, who wrote a play called *Emotional Creature*.

It speaks to the times when people say they are just *feeling emotional*.

They are trying to suppress their feelings while crying. No, you're not being emotional; instead we are all *always* emotional. When you're shutting down by crying, you're either sad, angry, frustrated, or lonely. Let's learn a deeper emotional intelligence in which we can actually name our feelings, moment to moment.

I hope that as we rise within a new paradigm, more and more people will understand that we're always emotional creatures.

Sometimes emotions flare, when we may feel:

- Elated
- Ecstatic
- Over the moon
- Sad
- Dismal
- Hopeless
- Fearful

Those are just spikes in the emotional spectrum.

I invite you, Gentle Reader, to look at that for yourself and catch yourself if you say you have to think your way through something to figure it out.

Go a little deeper, and say, "Let me feel into this, what's really here, what's under that."

So often, we're functioning above things. We've been taught to stuff our feelings. Very few people learn that the spectrum of human emotion is both real and something to be experienced. We can't navigate something if we aren't open to mapping it on some level.

We ultimately co-create with Spirit. Spirit, God, doesn't have to be defined by religion. You can define Spirit for yourself. I learned this in my twelve-step programs. You get to work with a god of your understanding. It can be the God you were taught to believe in. It can be multiple people, as in a twelve-step support group. It can be guardian angels. It need only make sense to you.

The question is, who or what is helping you?

I hope your experience has been that of a friendly universe. Something or someone is always watching over you. I know that to be true because I didn't want to be on the planet; I was kicking and screaming metaphorically, not wanting to be here. I was held here nonetheless.

I'm a recovering crack addict who's never been in a crack house, who never had to eat out of a dumpster, who never had to sell my body for my drug of choice. In hindsight, I knew right away that I'd been protected all those years when I didn't even want to be alive.

Imagine now that I, and I hope you, too, are choosing to be here on this planet and here in your body and here in your life more than ever before. If you allow yourself to be truly held, imagine the magic that can happen. Let that happen. Yeah, it might be scary at first, but know that you deserve it. Know that in your heart of hearts, you deserve love, you deserve to be and feel whole, mind, body, spirit. You deserve and need and truly can feel in alignment with mind, body, and spirit. Allow this for yourself. Give yourself the gift of coming home to you!

Everything I'm saying to you I'm saying to myself. I need constant reminders that there's a plan for my life, that there's a god of my understanding who loves me, that wants me to be me. In expressing me to my fullest, I'm expressing a piece of the god of my understanding to the fullest in that capacity because there's only one of me in the entire cosmos. That's true about you. There's only one of you.

Yeah, maybe another person has the exact same name as you—first, middle, and last—but they don't have your vibration. They don't have your tone. They don't have your personality. They don't have your way of looking at life. They don't have your specific gifts and talents.

Be you. Do you.

I'm finally giving myself permission to do the same. The amount of freedom that comes with that is huge. I'm no longer wrapped up in *do, do, do*. Instead I'm trying to *be, be, be*.

Today, I'm a human being, not a human doing.

I can let go of those to-do lists of the past that identified me, that made me feel worthy of taking up space.

In my neurotic past, I'd wake up in the morning, and my list would look like:

- ✓ Wake up.
- ✓ Consult to-do list.
- ✓ Breathe.
- ✓ Make coffee.
- ✓ Re-consult list.

I wrote down every single thing I did just so I could check it off and feel like I was living. I associated busyness with worth. It's the best I could do at that time. At this point in my life, I'm mindful about my list making. I only write down things as reminders or to help me stay organized. The days of assigning value to a two-hundred item things-to-do list are long gone.

There's a huge, growing number of like-minded and love-hearted souls on the planet. Find them. Claim your people. Create your tribe.

Next, don't let your dreams die. Don't let your dreams be too small. Don't get too comfortable with your dreams. If it feels that you're already living them but there's further you can go, go there. Trust this. Surround yourself with people who talk like this or talk the way that resonates with you and your truth and how and who you want to be in this world.

I'm going to end here because I could go on forever. I don't know you, but I already love you. I'm overflowing with gratitude. Thank you for sharing this time and space with me. Now, go out there and share your beautiful, ever-evolving authentic self with the world. The world needs you!

Next Steps

Visit my website: www.QuinnFontaine.com.

RESOURCES

Books:

The Artist's Way by Julia Cameron
Jeremy P. Tarcher/Perigee, Los Angeles, CA, 1992.

Spiritual Liberation by Michael Bernard Beckwith
Simon and Schuster, 2008.

You Are a Badass by Jen Sincero
Running Press, Philadelphia, PA, 2013.

The Four Agreements by Don Miguel Ruiz
Amber-Allen Pub. San Rafael, CA, 1997.

WEBSITES:

www.agapelive.com
(trans-denominational spiritual center)

www.hoffmaninstitute.org
(interpersonal retreat center)

www.life-healing.com
    (in-patient residential treatment center)

www.translifeline.org
    (transgender and gender-nonconforming suicide
    prevention hotline)

www.aa.org (alcoholics anonymous)

www.na.org (narcotics anonymous)

www.slaafws.org (sex and love addicts anonymous)

About the Author

Quinn Alexander Fontaine has a background in all things expressive: stand-up, sketch, and improvisational comedy; installation work; and found-object sculpture.

He began his studies in Communications Media at Simmons College in Boston and continued his education studying Performance/Video at the California College of the Arts in Oakland.

Fontaine went on to star in the independent feature *Some Prefer Cake*. He also co-wrote, co-produced, and co-starred with the sketch comedy troupe Nude Coffee, playing venues throughout the United States and Europe, most notably Edinburgh's International Fringe Festival.

Fontaine's first-ever one-person show *Learning to Stay* was selected for fellowship with The Global Center for Cultural Entrepreneurship. Fontaine's second solo show, aptly titled *Kathleen Fontaine: The Man, the Mystery!* played to sold-out audiences. He's currently working on his third show, *Hung Like a Seahorse: The Show-and-Tell Version*. He's also recently embarked on his inspirational comedy career.

He's mostly a happy guy.

Made in the USA
Columbia, SC
17 September 2017